M000086154

In memory of America;
in hope of her resurgence

PRAISE FOR

Memory Work: A Self and Family Portrait

"I feel like I'm reading Mark Twain...Brava! Brava!"
Marjory Moses, *artist/jeweler*

"The scenes emerge from a mist until the figures are solid, the characters filled out before the sentence is complete."
Kaia, *librarian*

"A testament to the goodness of people..."
Marsha L. Brown, *Cincinnati Reds fan*

"... a best seller in the making."
Emily Leslie, *singer /social worker*

"...a thoughtful, observant and entertaining writer."
Michael Woody, *musician, minister, scholar*

"I absolutely love these vignettes. Even now plotting a way to turn them into a play."
Helen Carlisle, *playwright.*

"The Thanksgiving and birthday details and dialogue were just the best."
Ruth Kennedy Cooke, *educator*

"I have enjoyed reading every bit of this."
Julie Parker Perry, *Gramma of twelve*

"Superb talents."
Stephen Stanley, *retired administrator*

"Yay!"
> Anita Hauenstein, *psychologist, minister, shaman*

"...heartwarming, real and poignantly written."
> Carol Starz, *astrologer*

"Loved the way this captured the thinking of a child."
> Helen Flores, *Scrabble parodist*

"This is so exciting! I want one."
> Eileen Johnson, *renowned baker*

"...captures the essence. Love the writing style."
> Jen Nice, *singer*

"Emily is a great writer."
> Daniel B. Cook, *conservative realtor*

MEMORY WORK:

A Self and Family Portrait

Emily Griffin Brodeur

MEMORY WORK: A SELF AND FAMILY PORTRAIT.
Copyright © 2020 by Emily Brodeur. All rights
reserved. Printed in the United States of America. No
part of this book may be used or reproduced without
written permission.

Library of Congress Cataloguing-in-Publication Data
has been applied for.

ISBN: 978-1-0878-8261-1

ii

Contents

Prologue

Today, April 8, 2020, the future of our democracy has been dealt another grievous, if not fatal blow. The US Supreme Court hurriedly convened remotely just in time to overturn a lower court ruling to delay an election, thus forcing the citizens of Wisconsin to go out in the midst of the Covid-19 pandemic to vote, or not. Mail-in ballots were not delivered on time, those sent back late will not be counted, and the vast majority of polling places were closed. Wily and predacious foxes have been installed in every agential henhouse upon which we most rely, and the watchdogs of our freedoms and our collective purse have been muzzled, poisoned, or cast out. The chief rabble-rouser, whose name will live in infamy, would seem to be profiteering on the misery of the people he was "elected" to serve.

But enough about him. He has taken up too much airspace and print already, and I will leave it to the historians to better chronicle his crimes. The carnage that is both here and coming, the suppression of voting and dissent, the bitterness of the divide between his supporters and the rest of us, will exact a toll far more grim than that of the virus itself.

Which reminds me of my father, who died on this day twenty-five years ago. He used to say, during the Cold War era, when everyone was building fallout shelters in anticipation of a Soviet nuclear attack, that he would not wish to be one of the survivors. I understand his point, given what looms ahead of us now. Thus, in commemoration of the anniversary of his death, I will begin my tale with him.

Chapter one

Knowledge of My Father

William Comer Griffin was born the son of a tenant farmer on August 18, 1913 in the tiny town of Castleberry, Alabama. His father was William Samuel Griffin, and his mother, born Annie Lou Williams, was a schoolteacher during his early life. This pattern of the women being more educated than the men was widespread on both sides of my family for several generations.

A red-haired, freckle-faced child, he went by the name Comer, pronounced "Coma," for the first few decades of his life. The name was in honor of a beloved public figure, Braxton Bragg Comer, who was governor of Alabama between 1907 and 1911. Governor Comer had championed the small farmer, protected small business, and helped to regulate the railroads.

Almost as soon as I could talk I began to pester my father to tell me what he could remember about his childhood. This was part of a personal investigation which I will later describe. He was remarkably unforthcoming on the subject, however. I knew he had had a doll named Don, and that his earliest ambition had been to have eleven children, all of them boys. He himself had had just two younger sisters, Mary Belle and Lois.

Most intriguing of all was his very brief description of finding himself, at about age four, lying in a ditch of rainwater looking into the large and frightening eyes of a frog. It seemed he was hiding, or had run away. When pressed to reveal just why he would be hiding in such a place, he became tight-lipped and anxious.

Much later in life I heard a few veiled references to the fact that Granddaddy Griffin had been an alcoholic in those years.

The story he most enjoyed telling was about his youthful complicity with grammar school bad boy...was it Neville Dickson? Though he could not recall their actual misdeeds, he rejoiced in recounting, again very briefly, how they had had to stay after school to write one hundred times, "The way of the transgressor is hard," and "Overcome evil with good."

Comer graduated from high school in 1931, just as the Great Depression had reached full swing. Later he would laugh as he sang, "Yes, we have no bananas. We have no bananas today." Stymied by poverty, he spent three years trying to earn the money to go to college by growing strawberries, which was the major export of his town. At the end of that time he had scraped together ten dollars. He went anyway.

It was the late summer of 1933 when he arrived at the University of Alabama in Tuscaloosa. I would have loved to have heard the details: how he got there, what he took with him, how he found his way to the abandoned observatory where he and three other young men

4

lived a kind of squatters' existence. What did they eat? What did they sleep on? He was too humiliated by his sojourn in dire straits to ever say.

He got a WPA job picking up trash on campus. "Franklin D. Roosevelt put me through college." I think I only heard him say that once. FDR was his hero, and, as he grew older, he even looked like him. Sometimes when I come across a photo of FDR in a history book I am startled by his resemblance to my dad.

He and my mother met in a physics class a few years later. Their first conversation took place in the hallway, and I'm sure she initiated it. He had his foot up on a radiator, was smoking a pipe, I think, and wearing a pair of white linen slacks— procured and kept clean at what personal sacrifice I can only imagine. A handsome young man.

They quickly discovered their common- alities: miraculously, they shared the same birthday, though my mother, then Lou Ellen Nettles, was already a graduate student and a year younger than he. She had graduated from Pine Hill High School at the age of fifteen in 1930, an inauspicious year to launch. To finance her trip to Birmingham and her enrollment in Birmingham- Southern College, she had borrowed one hundred dollars from the only man in town still drawing a paycheck: the mailman, Mr. Bo Sheffield. Like my father, she was deeply ashamed of the poverty that had forced her to take a job as a live-in babysitter and helper in the home of sociology professor, Dr. Elmer Bathurst and his wife, Ora

Belle. They were newly transplanted Midwesterners who found their introduction to southern culture in the era of breadlines both fascinating and horrifying. They were amazed that though there were no parental funds to help my mother, her parents still employed a cook at home. And even though the Bathursts and their two children remained lifelong friends, my mother was forever humiliated by having worked as a maid.

Chapter two

Beginning of a Family

In about 1938 when Comer, also known then as Red, arrived in Arlington, Alabama unannounced to call upon my mother, it caused a flurry of excitement in the town. At age twenty-three she was widely regarded as an old maid, having spent the three years after college graduation working and saving money to buy a house for her parents and younger siblings. This she had accomplished.

She had but a single item in her hope chest: a hand-crocheted tablecloth made by "Miss Benie" Dilger, from whom she had purchased an antebellum house and ten acres for the sum of one thousand dollars. For the tablecloth, which I still have, she paid twenty-five dollars to cover the cost of the thread.

The house had been in a state of disrepair, long unpainted and with no indoor plumbing or electricity. Her enterprising seventeen-year-old brother, James Dennis, known as Buddy, had taken on the task of wiring the house, and my grandfather, Samuel Cornelius Nettles, Sr., had done the plumbing. It was at the massive double front doors of this, the old Dumas house, that my father knocked and found the family not at home. A sharp-eyed neighbor spotted him and managed to detain him until they returned. "I wasn't going to let that good-looking young man get away!" she later said.

It was a long courtship, for those days, as my father needed first to get a job and pay off whatever debts he had incurred. They were married on June 18, 1941, at the Arlington Methodist Church, which was decorated with smilax and yucca. Mother had tried to insist that Daddy purchase a suit for his father, who otherwise would be too embarrassed to come to the wedding. Daddy had refused, and his father did not attend.

Six months later the Japanese attacked Pearl Harbor. When the announcement came on the radio my mother somehow managed to explode her first ever batch of Jello onto the ceiling of their tiny apartment in Montgomery. My father's job as a hydraulic engineer for the US Geological Survey was considered an essential service, and he was not required to enlist. When, a few years into the marriage, my mother had still not become pregnant, they tried artificial insemination. When that failed, they decided on adoption.

My brother, whose original name had been Michael Eugene Nelson, was a three-year-old living happily, from all I've heard, with a foster family. He was renamed William Michael Griffin. I have vague memories of hearing that he was of Greek descent. His entrance into their lives was a very happy time, though they shared their one-bedroom apartment with a Polish refugee.

8

On November 17, 1947, my sister Nancy Ellen was born. Uncle Buddy, whose medical education my mother had helped finance, had written a reassuring letter to his sister containing the evidence that even at the advanced age of thirty-three she could still hope to deliver a healthy child. Nancy weighed six pounds, 12 ounces, and was indeed a healthy baby.

Less than eight months after her birth she performed the jaw-dropping feat of uttering her first complete sentence, having chosen to remain silent until then. In protest of a serving of strained peas, she had picked up the bowl, and, looking at the dog, enunciated clearly, "I want to give Spot this." This may be the single most astounding thing that anyone in my family has ever done. Spot got the peas and Nancy still hates them.

Two years later my mother had a miscarriage, and in 1951 she was pregnant with me. The obstetrician kept telling her that I would be born much earlier in the year than my sister and would be much smaller. She did not believe him, and told him I would be born on the same day and weigh exactly the same thing. On November 16, 1951, the day before my sister's birthday, the doctor induced labor. Mother said he had a fishing trip scheduled. Having to be right, apparently, he recorded my birth weight as six pounds, 11 and 3/4 ounces. My sister and I always believed ourselves to be twins, separated by the accident of four years and the doctor's interference.

Six weeks later we moved to Walla Walla, Washington. My father drove up ahead, and Mother and the three of us children followed on the train. It was January, and the swirling snow was a novelty for all. Mother said I would laugh as the snowflakes hit my face when we traveled from one train car to another. Not long after we arrived, however, I came down with a serious case of pneumonia. Penicillin and sunshine through a window saved my life.

My first memory that contains my father is of being at a family camp somewhere in Washington when I was twenty-one months old. My sister and I were playing on a swing set, and Daddy came to call us to dinner. We wanted him to push us on the swings. (It was at least two more years before I mastered the art of pumping a swing myself.) He calmly declined. My sister said, "Then we'll run away." He pointed out that it was raining, and indeed a few cold drops were beginning to fall. Nancy then plucked two large leaves from a vine that was twining up one post of the swing set and said, "Come on, Emily. These will be our umbrellas."

Was she insane? The prospect of wandering into the cold, dark woods with nothing but a leaf and a five-year-old to protect me was an alarming proposition. "You'll get mighty hungry," Daddy said, reasonably.

"No we won't! We won't run away," I said.

I have just one other memory from that camp, which follows shortly, along with an explanation of why I bothered to retain these things at all. And before that, just one earlier memory, extracted from the mists of time a few weeks prior to this, and a memory of a memory, though the original is lost.

Chapter three

The Smiling Black Man

My earliest memory, mostly kinetic and visual, is of being tossed into the air and caught by a large, smiling black man. My mother was standing to the side pleading with him to stop, but he did it again and again, to my squealing delight. My sense is that it was the most thrilling thing I had ever experienced in my short life.

The location was the bottom of the steps leading up to the well porch of my grandparents' house in Arlington, the house that still legally belonged to my mother. The man, I was able to ascertain many years later, was really an older teenager. His name was Samson Dumas, and he was my mother's informally adopted brother.

My grandparents, Neil (or Neal) Nettles and his wife, Janie Maude Rikard Nettles, had taken Samson in when he was eight. His mother was dead, and his father, Badge Dumas, was very ill and sensed that he had only a short time left to live. Though accounts vary, I was told that he brought Samson to my grandfather and asked if he would take him in and raise him "and teach him what he needs to know to be a man." Papa Neil said that he would. A hand-written note was brought to give it some semblance of legality. The note said, "I give this here boy to Mr. Neil and Mr. Sam." Sam was my mother's older brother,

Samuel Cornelius Nettles, Jr., and he owned the sawmill where Badge was employed.

Samson was the third of three young black boys whom my grandparents took in. The first was Robert Bob, known as Brutus, who had committed a crime. He and a twelve-year-old girl had stolen a quarter from the Post Office with the intent to buy chewing gum. This was considered a federal offense. On the day that the feds showed up "to take him to prison," so my mother said, my grandfather met them at their car. "You're not taking him," he informed them. "He did something naughty, but he's not a criminal. If you lock him up, he'll become one." Brutus was, at the time, a tiny eight-year-old, and his mother, Henrietta Bob, was very sick with tuberculosis. He was clinging to Papa Neil's pants leg in terror, I believe.

The feds hedged a bit. "Someone's got to take him into custody. Who's going to do that, you?" one asked, jeeringly. Papa Neil said that he would. Perhaps some paperwork was signed.

William Henry, the Uncle Bill I never met, brought home the next boy. Bill, at age seventeen, had dark, wavy hair and was the Wilcox County heart-throb. The Depression was raging, and though most people down there could grow their own food, times were hard. He had started his own little business delivering candy and other supplies to small country stores.

When he arrived at one such store, perhaps in Magnolia, a twelve-year-old black boy approached him. "I'm hungry, boss. Would you give me something to eat?"

Uncle Bill inquired into the circumstances. The boy, Tony Jane Hannah, explained that he had been put out by his family because they said he ate too much.

"Hop in," said Uncle Bill. "We have plenty to eat at my house. You can live with us." Papa Neil later drove over to see the family and check out the story. They had just had another baby and resources were stretched too thin. So he told Tony he could live with them on one condition: he had to agree to finish high school.

Bill died of sepsis just a few years later, shortly before Penicillin became available. Brutus and Tony also died very young, both by accidental drowning. All of the losses hit the family very hard.

Samson thrived, however, and made his way to California, where, for a time, he was out of touch. An accidental encounter brought him back in touch with the family. My cousin Bragg, known by then as Dan, had moved to California with his wife Angela, nee Torres. An Oakland police officer was moonlighting doing security at their apartment complex. That officer was Samson, and the connection was renewed. When Aunt Mildred, my mother's younger sister, and her husband Dan Cook visited, they got together.

Samson insisted on taking them to the police station to meet his fellow officers. "Y'all! Y'all! This is my sister! We grew up together! When I was eight-years-old, my daddy gave me to her daddy." I can imagine that the wording of that last sentence took his colleagues somewhat aback. And it was an anomaly, to say the least, that the sister of such a black man would turn out to be the President-General of the International United Daughters of the Confederacy.

I had always wondered whether Tony, Brutus and Samson had felt like members of the family or more like live-in help. About Tony and Brutus, I cannot say, but Samson supplied an answer, and twenty years ago, another.

In 1999, my sister was spending a few days in Arlington taking care of Mother—something we both did periodically to give her helpers, Shirley and Lyda, a break, since otherwise they had no time off. There was a knock at the front door and Nancy answered to find a large black man smiling at her confidently.

"I bet you know who *this* is."

She did. "Samson?" She had not seen him since she was five-years-old.

"That's right."

She invited him in and he gestured expansively in the wide, high-ceilinged hallway. "This is my home," he said. "I grew up in this house. Your grandparents took me in and raised me as their own child. They taught me everything I needed to know to make it in the world. How to plant a garden, how to sew on a button, how to cook...They made me what I am today. I bet you've seen that picture." He again looked at her expectantly.

She knew exactly what picture he was talking about. It was a black and white photograph of a line of eight or nine men in hats staring grimly at the camera, as photographic subjects were wont to do in those days. They were my grandfather's fox-hunting companions, and all of them except him, I understand, had at some point been members of the Ku Klux Klan. Papa Neil alone is seated, in a chair in the center. Samson is sitting on his lap.

Chapter four

Undertaking My Study

It had been shortly after my memorable first and last encounter with Samson that we went to the camp in Washington.

There is only one other thing from that that I remember: driving down a road, bordered by tall trees, sitting in the back seat with Nancy and Mama. Mike was the first, I believe, to spot a flying squirrel, which set off a wave of excitement. Everyone else was able to see it, but I had no idea what a squirrel was, or even where to look. Mother tried to point, but I didn't know how to follow the direction of a pointing finger, and demanded to know what it was that I was supposed to see.

Nancy explained that it was sort of like a cat. Mother said, "Look up! Look up!" and I looked straight up but was still denied a vision of this fabulous apparition, some kind of cat with wings. I howled with frustration at being left out.

In the weeks that followed, as we settled into our new house in Tacoma, the events that occurred at camp were frequently discussed. There was The Great Archery Contest, in which my father won first place, shooting a bullseye on his first attempt. Most important, it seemed, was the Family Talent Show, in which our entry had been "The Shrinking and Growing Machine." My sister and I had been dressed in identical dresses, and as my mother turned the crank on one side of a large box, I would walk in and my sister would exit the other side. Then reverse. My father and brother had also been identically attired, and performed the same operation.

No matter how many times I heard these things described and tried to picture them, I could not recall them. Even after receiving a major clue, that Nancy and I had been wearing our homemade pink and white-striped dresses, with which I was quite familiar, I was completely unable to do anything but imagine. I honestly could remember nothing, even at such a short remove, but my failure to see the marvelous flying cat, and the part about the swing set and the leaf umbrellas. Since those two memories were all I had left, I resolved to hang onto them and make sure that I never again fell into such a void of recollection.

Having entered the scene now as a sentient, remembering being, it will be impossible for me to describe events in advance of this from any point of view other than my own.

But it was not just my own lapse of memory that troubled me. It was the fact that older people could not recall having been my age, judging from the incomprehensible explanations they so frequently gave, and their inability to decipher what I was trying to convey. Bear in mind, I lacked the words then, but had the concepts. Further confirmation of the seriousness of the divide came a few weeks later in the form of visitors who arrived on a gray, Sunday afternoon.

Afternoon Visitors

There was a knock at the door, and my father opened it. He greeted the couple on the porch with an air of surprised bonhomie and invited them in. Apparently the man worked in Daddy's office, and he and his wife had dropped by to welcome us to Tacoma. The man was in a suit and the woman was wearing slacks, which was wrong to do on Sunday.

It was time for my nap, and my mother was getting ready to carry me upstairs. "Oh, look at the baby," the woman said. "Isn't she adorable?" My mother pulled me back a little, as if she didn't want her to touch me. I was confused by this, and fixed the woman with an appraising stare.

"That is the strangest look I've ever seen on a baby's face," the lady said. My mother didn't seem to like this word, strange. "Wouldn't you love to know what goes on in their little heads?" the visitor continued. "And wouldn't it be wonderful to be that age, to remember it? But of course, you can't. No one can."

"No, of course not," my mother politely agreed.

I was shocked that my mother was agreeing with what this lady said even though she didn't like her. I felt certain that they were wrong, and that it could be done. I believe the word "discovery" had been uttered earlier in the day, perhaps by Mike, and I had some sense of what it might mean. This was going to be mine, I decided, and someday I would prove it—that continuity of consciousness could be maintained from very early childhood.

Fifty years later I asked my mother, "Who were the people who came to the door one Sunday afternoon not long after we moved to Tacoma?"

"I'm surprised you remember that! The man worked in Bill's office."

"You were uncomfortable with the woman. Why was that?"

"Oh. They had been drinking."

I hadn't known that, hadn't recognized that smell. That explained her mistrust and why she held me back.

My first theory concerning the widespread and disturbing discontinuity of memory was that adults and small children were two different species, but this one was quickly discarded after seeing a few photos: my father, fat and swaddled in a baby carriage, then dressed in white as a toddler with his sister, Mary Belle; my mother as an infant staring seriously ahead. I was willing to take their word that these were, in fact, themselves.

My second was that there might be a certain age at which previous memory was wiped out in some sort of ceremony of forgetting. Joining the church seemed the most likely candidate for this, and when Mike joined the Methodist Church at age ten, I was excited about having the opportunity to check this out.

"Do you still remember anything that happened last week?" I asked.

He found the question insulting in the extreme. "Don't be a moron," he replied.

My study continued, the members of my nuclear family my unwitting study subjects. Daddy, as I've said, was sadly a disappointment in this regard, as was Mike. I knew he had been adopted at age three and was surprised that he could remember nothing of his previous life. He had little interest in even discussing what he could remember of the year they lived in Washington, D.C. where he had gotten to participate in a Fourth of July parade, or the time they had lived in the house with five bedrooms and all the glass doors.

My interviews with Nancy and Mama were much more fruitful. Nancy remembered being at a tea party with my mother when she was two and the women there being so wrapped up in admiring the outfit she was wearing that she felt invisible, as if she were nothing but a suit of clothes. She remembered playing in Spot's doghouse when she was two.

My mother remembered their house burning down when she was two.

"What were you wearing?" I asked.

"It was night. I'm sure I was in a gown."

"What color was it?"

"Oh, probably white."

"No, not *probably*! Do you remember it?"

"And George, the colored man, ran back into the kitchen, and all he came out with was a bowl of clabber. Not any of Mama's good china or silver." She recites the story in the familiar way.

"But do you remember it, or is it just what you were told?" I was practically crying with frustration, trying to get her to see the distinction.

She didn't like my tone. "Don't dispute with me," she said. "If you act like that, I'm not going to tell you any more."

But she relented. She remembered sitting on a wooden horse when she was two, saying, "Go, Gillie, go."

Was that *it*?

Finally I was able to solve the enigma. The difference between retaining early memories and not retaining them had nothing to do with gender differences, and there was no certain age of demarcation. Nor did it have that much to do with any innate capability. Nancy and Mama clearly had it, but had preserved only these few fleeting snapshots from the time when they were like me. The problem was simply that they had not decided to do it, that they had not considered it important. Clearly the task was left to me.

My field of endeavor was at first overly broad, in that it included observing and preserving a mental record of EVERYTHING. This included the patterns of color I would see when I pressed my fists to my eyeballs, the play of color on a shaft of dust motes in the sunlight, the shrinking and wrinkling of a yellow telephone company balloon in the corner of our bedroom closet. The amount of data soon swamped my limited capacity for storage, and I decided to limit my efforts to only those events and observations that were especially interesting to me.

Chapter five

Lamb Chops for Breakfast

Lack of context and attention span made retaining sequences particularly difficult, as the following example will show:

I sauntered into the kitchen the morning of my second birthday. "Happy birthday," one of my siblings said. Though I had been forewarned, I had no idea what a birthday was, other than that it was special and for me. That and becoming entitled to hold up two fingers instead of one.

Mike, then ten, was full of excitement. "Guess what your surprise is?"

"Mike," Mother said warningly, meaning he was not supposed to give it away.

"Give up? Okay, I'll give you a hint. Lamb chops!" he shouted, barely daunted.

"We're having lamb chops for breakfast?" Everyone laughed to hear me say that and I was proud that I seemed to have guessed correctly.

"Emily probably thinks that lamb chops are something white and fluffy," snickered Nancy.

"I do not!" I was fully aware that lamb chops, much favored by the rest of my family, were a difficult gray meat, and though I could not yet see the appeal, I was prepared, in the face of their celebratory mood, to keep an open mind. Nevertheless, I formed the mental image of something white and fluffy as I marched with aplomb to the oven to check the accuracy of my guess.

I pulled open the oven door, as if I had been doing this every day of my life. Mother was horrified. "Don't ever, ever touch the oven door!"

"Never? Not even when I grow up?" This was a serious question. I knew there was the expectation that I would become a larger child and then a grownup, and I was pondering the ramifications of being forever forbidden to cook. Fortunately, Mother could tell that I was not just being sassy, and even she was amused.

Just before the oven door slammed shut I caught a glimpse of something wrapped in foil on the center rack. The lamb chops, I presumed.

Fade to black, and cut to later that afternoon. A weak November light barely illuminated the dining room. On the dark oak table was the pale green birthday cloth, around which sat mothers holding whiny, squirming babies. I was one of them. My mother kept trying to feed me cake, but I wanted ice cream. Ice cream! She finally told me I could have some if I promised to eat some cake. I would agree to anything as long as I got some ice cream first.

For years I was convinced that we had lamb chops for breakfast on my second birthday, that this was the special treat to mark the day. No one else could recall that at all. The memorable thing for the rest of them was that my mother had won a cake in a raffle—a white cake in the shape of a lamb.

And it was years before I could put two and two together: that my brother's lamb chop clue concerned the cake, and that it was this special cake that my mother was so eager to have me consume. My two-year-old understanding could form only the most primitive of equations: that lamb chop equaled lamb chop. The subtleties of the constant hints and clues with which my older siblings supplied me were completely lost on me. While everyone else was celebrating the perfect birthday cake, I was celebrating (wrongly) having for once guessed something right.

The morning and the afternoon were like two separate days—two shards of memory joined only by archaeological reconstruction…which was probably better for my self-esteem. Had I been able to maintain concentration long enough to not only notice the lack of lamb chops, but the later appearance of something white and fluffy, as my sister had predicted I'd be idiotic enough to expect, I probably would have felt like a complete dope. Instead I felt wonderfully sharp and mature as I contemplated the prospect of an oh-so-very grown up breakfast, and a future of never touching the oven door.

An even more daunting task of reassembly awaited me, one that took over fifty years to complete.

Chapter six

Open House

We were cruising in our baby blue Studebaker down the wide, tree-lined streets of the Tacoma suburbs. I was standing on the bump on the backseat floorboard, which was my favorite spot in the whole car.

"Y'all better behave when we get there," Mama cautioned. "Remember whose pumpkins you are."

Mike was the only one of us who had changed clothes after church. In honor of the formality of the occasion he had switched into his blue Cub Scout uniform with the nifty bright yellow neck scarf that was cinched with a little gold clasp.

"Yeah," he warned, giving me and my sister a sarcastic look. "Remember whose *bumpkins* you are."

Was it bumpkins or pumpkins? Which one was good? We were going to an *Open* House. Open, house! Open, sesame! Was it a house without a front? "How do you open a house?" I asked.

"You just open the door and walk in, stupid. What's the matter? Haven't you ever gone in a door before?" This was mean, but it was still funny. Mike was already sick of Nancy and me, and we'd barely even gotten started.

"Now Mr. Adams is the chairman of the building committee, isn't he? And Mrs. Adams, I believe she's on the pastor parish relations committee, isn't that right?" Daddy asked Mama. "Guess we better mind our p's and q's."

Being made to recite the alphabet was a worrying prospect. I only knew A, B, C and D. And sometimes E, F, G. I pictured our family lined up on a doorstep being made to recite the alphabet as a kind of rite of passage. Everyone else would pass with flying colors but I'd make a total fool of myself. Would they kick our whole family out then, or only me?

"Hey Emily, guess what? When we get there we can act very proper. We can say, 'Hello, madam,'" Nancy said in a fake proper voice.

This was very funny.

"Hello, madam," she says again. "And how are you today? My, don't you look lovely."

I was laughing my head off. "Madam Adam," I say, trying it out.

"Hey, that's pretty good, Emily! It even rhymes."

"Madamadam, madamadam, madamadam," I chanted.

Mike tried ostentatiously to ignore us.

"Hey, wouldn't it be funny if her name was Eve? You know, like Adam and Eve?" Nancy suggested.

Mama and Daddy were still talking in the front seat, reviewing what they knew about our hosts. "We'll just try to act like white folks," Daddy said softly.

"Oh, Daddy," Mama scolded.

Nancy leaned over and whispered to me, "Hey Emily! Did you know that Adam and Eve were naked? They didn't even wear underpants, and they were grownups."

Wow! "Do Mama and Daddy know?"

"Sure," she shrugged, with a worldly nonchalance. "Everybody knows about Adam and Eve. You're not going to believe this part. You know what they were wearing?"

"I thought they weren't wearing anything."

"Just this one thing... Aprons!"

This was too much. "Even the man?" I asked, incredulously. We collapsed into mirth.

"You better shut up or I'm telling," Mike warned, with a mature, knowing look.

I pictured a house that was open at the front like a dollhouse with people wearing nothing but aprons moving from room to room. Must be some kind of very weird party we were going to. It sure sounded different from the birthday cake and balloon affairs I had encountered up till then.

They Let Us In

My first disappointment was that it was just a regular house, only bigger. We fought over who got to push the doorbell, and I was selected for the honor. Daddy lifted me up to perform this novel operation. "Ding dong," we said. But the real sound it made was completely different. It didn't have any words.

A man and a lady wearing clothes opened the door. Another letdown. "You're the Griffins, aren't you?" the lady asked. "I'm so delighted that all of you could come. I guess I should say 'y'all,' shouldn't I? Aren't you from Alabama?"

Nancy nudged me to make sure I took note of the proper talking.

We were all duly named and exhibited, and the lady stooped down to my level. "Hello, sweetheart."

"Hello, madam," I responded gravely.

Her head snapped back up toward my parents. Nancy was growing restive and anxious, trying not to laugh. She never really expected me to go through with it. Mother seemed mortified by my weird behavior.

Sensing the anxiety, I tried to amend my faux pas. "I mean, Madam Adam."

"Is she a dwarf?" The lady seemed to be making a joke, but Mama and Daddy didn't get it. "What I meant was, this child can't possibly be as young as she looks."

Mother relaxed a little. "She turned two in November," she said proudly.

Good news. I was not a dwarf. I seized the opportunity that this prolonged attention granted me. "Did you know that your door was closed?"

"Why, yes."

"Because I thought this was supposed to be an *Open* House."

This made my parents nervous. I was talking like a smart aleck, and hadn't said ma'am even once. But the lady laughed gaily.

34

"You look lovely today, madam," I said, on parrot-delay, wanting to make sure to work it all in.

This charmed her. "So serious, isn't she? And so polite. This is truly remarkable."

The words began to fly over my head. "Have you considered...You really ought to…"

And from Mama, "Down home we always just...My brother Buddy said…"

We were permitted to enter, mercifully without having to recite the alphabet. A big relief.

In The Foyer

The attention stayed on me. I was basking in the sense of being special, of being the trick pony in the center of the ring, and was amazed at all the hoopla that proper speech seemed to generate. Nancy jabbed me jealously and I knew I had it coming. After all, she was the one who taught me all this stuff and I was getting all the credit.

"And Nancy Ellen, when she was only seven or eight months old, picked up her bowl of strained peas and said, 'I want to give Spot this.'"

"Yes," said the lady, turning briefly to survey my six-year-old sister in her little brown coat, brown braids, brown velveteen muff. "I'm sure she must be very bright also."

Mike stood, smiling stiffly, being completely ignored. No one said a word about his uniform.

She turned her gaze back on me, the blonde-haired baby. "It's not really necessary for you to call me madam," she smiled.

35

"Then maybe I should call you Eve."

She looked confused.

"You're married to Adam, aren't you?"

Oh. Ha ha ha. The grownups laughed at my joke that wasn't a joke. "We may look like it, but we're really not *that* old."

"You're a dope," Nancy hissed instructively. "Adam and Eve are dead! That was only in the Bible."

But I knew what she was really worried about. She was afraid I'd say the part about no underwear. I wasn't that stupid.

The hostess turned to me seriously, dropping the baby voice. "Adams is our last name. My husband's first name is ____, and my first name is Alice. You may call me that, if you like."

"You've changed a lot," I said, looking her over.

"Oh? What do you mean?"

By this point my parents were starting to look very worried.

"You don't look like your picture."

"Where did you see my picture, sweetheart?" She and my parents conferred. Could I possibly have seen it in the church newsletter? Such a tiny photo, all those committee members. Did I really read the church newsletter?

"Oh no, she doesn't read. We don't believe in pushing our children."

But maybe I could read, if I tried. That was an exciting thought.

"What picture, honey?" she asked again.

"When you were a little girl! You look different now." I was still not making myself clear. "Do you still have the blue dress?" I tried to picture her in the outfit. "I liked your hair when it was long."

I felt our hostess shiver with fascination. "But there's only one portrait of my brother and me when we were small. A blue dress? That was a white one, I think. You know how they always dressed girls in white. And my hair was always kept short."

She and my mother started talking about people who had died, and they seemed to think I might have hooked up with one of them. Mrs. Adams leaned in, not wanting to miss a word of my revelation. "Tell me what you see, darling. Tell me everything you see."

This made Daddy very angry. Who was he mad at, me? If it was the lady he was mad at, he seemed to lack the power or the will to intervene. "That's enough now, hear?" he muttered, directing his words to Mama.

"I don't see it now," I whined rudely. I was frustrated by the effort of trying to make myself understood. "I saw your picture before, lots of times, when you were in the book."

Nancy, as usual, was the only one who got it, and she generously stepped in to help me out. "*Alice In Wonderland*," she translated. "That's the book she means."

Trills of delighted laughter, mixed with my father's sound, relief.

"So would you like to call me Alice?"

My parents stiffened uncertainly. Southern protocol forbade a child to call an adult by her first name unless it was preceded by a title like "Miss" or "Cousin." But here in the great, freer-wheeling Northwest they were slightly off their footing.

"Cousin Alice?" my mother suggested hopefully.

Noting their discomfort, our hostess added, "Or you may call me Mrs. Adams."

I was not insensible of the honor I was accorded and was thrilled to be taken so seriously. I sensed the swirling currents of parental anxiety, but capitulating to "Mrs. Adams" was way too boring to endure. I tried to see her as Alice, but could only get as far as envisioning her in the white stockings and black shoes. I was completely unable to redo her head. I could sort of see her as the Original Woman, though, and I pictured her naked with a secret, guilty glee.

"I think I'd rather just call you Eve."
Nancy laughed.

Going Upstairs

This had all been fascinating to me, and as the grownups negotiated turning me over to my new champion for a special tour, I resolved to remember all of this, every word possible, so as not to betray my current self once I reached the age of Eve.

"I've got something to show you that I think you'll really like," she said mysteriously.

Just being handed over to a stranger was in itself almost unheard of, but, oh boy! I could hardly wait. My hope grew that this different kind of grownup was going to answer some of my most pressing questions, like whether there were really goblins, or God. It was about time.

She led me across the living room to a staircase. "I have a little girl, too."

"Do I get to play with her?"

"Oh, she's not here, honey. And she's not little anymore." I heard the tone of longing and regret.

My left foot joined my right foot on the first step, and I tested the nap of the thick carpet with the toe of my white high-topped shoe. She was beaming at me. "But she used to be tiny like you."

I was eager to get started on solving the mysteries of life. "Well, what about goblins?" I asked.

She stopped. "What about them, sweetie? There aren't any goblins here. Don't be frightened."

"So are they real?" Mike had always said they were, and Nancy went along with it—skinny white ones with red eyes that lived in our basement behind the rollaway bed cabinet. I had never succeeded in seeing one, despite my regular checking.

"Oh no, they're not real. Don't worry."

"I'm not worried. I *wish* they were real. I want to see one."

This gave her pause.

"So I guess God's not real then either, huh?" I was no sucker.

"Oh yes, dear! God is very, very real. You must always believe that."

One foot, two foot. One foot, two foot. "Then where is He?"

"Oh, He's everywhere. He's everywhere at once."

I hated that answer. We reached the top.

She pushed open the first door with a flourish, and I was looking into a flowery girl's room as big as our living room at home. There were rows and rows of stuffed animals and expensive-looking dolls. I had never seen such a display, such a static museum of childhood. The room looked impossibly orderly, unlived in.

"Is she dead?" I asked in horror.

"What? Is *who* dead?" She looked over at the fancy dolls and went in and plucked one from the shelf. "See? It's only a doll. It's not real."

"I *know* dolls aren't real. I mean your daughter. Is she dead?" It was abundantly clear to me that this kid was way farther gone than just down the street at a friend's house. Dead equaled gone, I'd been told, and in my book dead also meant somebody killed you. It occurred to me that my charming hostess might have lured me up here to reenact the crime. I wondered if my parents were in on it and if even Nancy knew...that I was being sacrificed to the Rich People so our parents could fit in. They might not really be in favor of going through with it, but it sure seemed like you had to give this lady what she wanted, even if it was me. At this, I started to cry.

Mistaking my tears for compassion, she knelt to embrace me. "Oh no, dear, no! She's not dead! Don't say that." I felt her fear that I might in fact Know Something. It was that whole dead-people-picture thing again. "She's just big! Big like a grownup."

"Then why," I snuffled disconsolately, "does she play with all these teddy bears?" I was starting to believe that Eve might not be a killer, but it still didn't all add up. I knew there were big people who played with toys, and I started to calm down as I struggled to retrieve a really impressive term: Mongolian Idiot.

"Is she, you know...that kind of idiot?"

That did it. She jerked back up to her full height. "Well, she may not be a genius, but she's certainly no idiot! The idea! What have they been telling you at home?"

"They didn't tell me. I figured it out myself," I said proudly, despite her apparent ire. I was dying to discuss this, even if it meant a scolding. I knew Mongolian Idiots were real, but I'd never actually met one. Maybe if I played my cards right...

"Listen, my daughter...It's not very nice, calling people idiots. She does not play with teddy bears. She used to, a long time ago." At last she started to calm down.

I was a little disappointed, and still not buying it. "But they're all new."

"No, they are *not* new!" She walked over to the dresser and picked up a worn, stuffed monkey. "This was her favorite. He's not new."

She held the monkey out to me, precious bone to a strange talking dog. Despite being repulsed by its leer and its huge red grin, I accepted it gingerly, examining it for clues.

"But where is she?"

"She's away at school."

"But it's Sunday. You don't go to school on Sunday."

"She's in college. She has to stay there, even on Sunday."

"Why? Was she bad? Is she in jail?" Maybe I had been wrong about the whole thing. Maybe it was the daughter who had killed somebody.

"No! She wasn't bad. I told you, she's in college."

"I know, but is it in a jail? They won't let her out, even on Sunday? Did *she* kill somebody?" I asked.

Eve laughed a little and took a deep breath. She launched into an explanation of the educational system—the different levels, kinds of degrees, school holidays.

I was utterly bored by all of that and began to fidget inattentively.

"Do you have to go to the bathroom?"

"No!" And no one was even there to make me say, "no ma'am."

I Am Returned

We had reached the limit of our discourse. Eve took me back downstairs and returned me to my mother, with whom she tried to share her serious concern.

"Emily Jane is an unusual child," she began.

"Unusual!" Mother flinched, and I felt the alarm jolt through her.

"She wanted to see a goblin, she said she didn't believe in God...she kept talking about jail. She called my daughter an idiot."

Mother gave me a little shake.

"You know, you really must be careful of the things she hears you say. Children are so impressionable at this age."

"You mean she's not *normal*?"

This apparently was the worst of fates, worse even than being a Mongolian or a smart aleck. Stung by the criticism, Mother began a kind of collapse. "She never talks about these things at home! I certainly never told her anything about goblins. She doesn't know a thing about jails, of course not! I try so hard, way off up here by myself."

I had had no idea that Mama was so unhappy.

Eve relented and patted her soothingly on the arm. "Of course you do, dear. She's just very bright. That's all."

So was that a Good Thing or a Bad Thing? It was way, way past my nap time and I whined crankily to go home. I was just glad Eve didn't tell on me for not saying "ma'am."

Challenging Task

The grand and glorious scheme of permanent recollection that I had hatched there in the foyer was stymied by my almost total lack of narrative skill. I was also missing helpful bits of information such as the fact that there could be more than one person in the world with the same first name; and I had no tools useful for recording, like the alphabet.

That Sunday afternoon, so interesting, so whole in the moment, soon shattered like a dismantled jigsaw puzzle, the pieces disappearing under the couch, put back in the wrong boxes and lost in moves. My parents had been greatly discomfited by the whole ordeal, and this event never made it into the compendium of family stories. Children smarting off to grownups was not celebrated, the proscription of which I seemed to run continually afoul.

There was only one mention of it made in my hearing. "Why'd that woman think that Emily Jane was a DWAWF?" Mother asked plaintively. "Her head's not too big for her body!"

Efforts at retrieval and confirmation were also impeded by my inability to formulate the right questions. "Who was the lady named Eve who went to our church in Tacoma?" (There was no one by that name in that church.) "You know, the one with the mentally retarded daughter?" (No such person.)

It was not until I pulled up the mental image of the *Alice in Wonderland* shoes and stockings that I was able to recall her actual name. That was fifty or so years later, when I was about the same age as my unfortunate hostess had been at the time. Reassembly proceeded rapidly after that.

"Oh yes," said my mother, then eighty-seven. "Alice Adams. She had a brother who was very supercilious. She died of cancer after we left Tacoma when you were six."

There was only one other episode of similar length from early childhood that I made the effort to mentally record and keep. That was my visit some eighteen months later to a psychologist who was tasked with evaluating me for kindergarten readiness. This, too, was very novel and involved a kind of conversation that I otherwise never had with adults. My overall assessment of him had been charitable, despite his undeniable lack of skill.

Chapter seven

My Evaluation

It's the late summer of 1955, a few months before my fourth birthday. My mother, Nancy and I are in a waiting room of an office building, and it is all very strange. There is no nurse or receptionist to greet us, and I look in vain for the familiar jar of suckers. After a few minutes a man in a suit comes out of an adjoining room and greets us, obviously expecting us. He then asks me to come *alone* and follow him to his office.

This is absolutely unprecedented in my experience. I have never before been allowed to go anywhere alone with a strange man. My first thought, naturally, is that I am going to be killed. My mother is clearly anxious, and I don't know how to read this. Guilty conscience, perhaps? Whatever is about to happen, she is clearly in on it. She's the one who brought me here. Nancy, who is seven, nudges me and tells me to go ahead. "It's okay," she whispers.

"Don't say 'okay,' Nancy," Mama instructs. "Okay" is bad because it's slang, but my mother is fighting a losing battle against it. At this moment Nancy's "okay" is the only thing I trust.

"Okay," I say, cheekily. I get up and go.

The man closes the office door behind us and directs me to sit in a chair next to his desk. I climb up on it, disappointed that it's not the kind of chair office chair that twirls around. It seems he wants me to perform some kind of operations on his desk, but I can barely reach the top of it, which seems to throw him off. "Do you have a phone book?" I ask.

He seems shocked by my question. "Why? Do you need to make a call?"

"No, to *sit* on." This is what I always do in places with big chairs. He piles up some books, and I ask him to lift me up on top of the pile. He does it awkwardly, seeming embarrassed by the need to do so. "Don't you have a little girl?" I ask.

This question, too, seems to make him uncomfortable. "No," he answers in a clipped tone. "Just boys. A lot older than you." He clearly wants to drop the subject, though I would like to hear more about where they are, how old they are and whether he still has any of their toys around. I can't quite place what's different about him. Is he sad? Is he shy? (I think I asked him this.) In any case, he has not given the usual polite reply, which is, "No, but I *wish* I had a little girl."

"Do you go to our church?" I ask, church being the usual haunt of men in suits, as far as I know. I am trying to figure out what his connection to us is, what it is that supposedly makes it okay for me to be in a room alone with him. But no, he does not go to our church and has no wish to discuss his religious affiliation with me. What he *does* want is to take control of the interview.

He asks how old I am and I hold up three fingers and say "three." He tells me I can answer the question without holding up any fingers. I have never considered this possibility before, and I try it. It feels strange.

Next he asks if I know how to write my name. Easy! Piece of cake! "Do you have a crayon?" I inquire.

He does not. He places a piece of paper in front of me and hands me a grown-up writing implement — a ballpoint pen, perhaps—but he is alarmed by my grasp and the apparent pressure I intend to apply, and scrounges up a number 2 pencil instead. I manage to scrawl EMILY. I am quite pleased with my accomplishment, but he immediately shoots it down and starts lecturing me about "capital letters" and "small letters." Who knew? This is very interesting and I can hardly wait to tell Nancy and Mike. (Later it turns out that they had known about this all along and had just been keeping it from me.) Then he asks me if I can write, get this, my "sir name."

"I don't have one of those," I respond. What can he possibly mean by this? The name of someone whom one would normally address as "sir"? "You mean, like 'Daddy'?" I ask. "'Daddy' is not his real name," I add for clarification. The thought that this strange person has me confused with an adult male is amusing. I giggle. "I'm a girl," I point out.

"Yes, your name that is the same as your father's name. Your *last* name," he adds, finally divining the source of my confusion.

"Oh, I don't have to do that," I claim, meaning that this is not something that is required of me at home. "Nancy can do it. Ask her."

"You *will* have to do it," he says somewhat sharply. "And Nancy won't always be around."

This is a frightening thought. "Why not? What's going to happen to her?" Maybe my first suspicion was incorrect. Maybe Nancy, instead of me, is the one they're going to kill. I ask to be excused so I can tell her.

This is getting out of hand for him. "Soon you will go to school and you and Nancy will be in different classes. You'll have to do things for yourself."

I'm not sure I believe him. First he thought I was a man, and now with the mention of school he seems to have me confused with my older siblings. He writes my last name on a piece of paper and asks me to copy it. As far as I'm concerned, his printing all fits the description of "small letters." I make a wild stab at copying "Griffin"—though I believe he spelled it "Griffen," and soon give up. "I don't have to do that," I again assert, meaning that not only has this never been required of me before, but I can't imagine a circumstance in which such a task would be assigned.

He doesn't like my answer.

He then brings out a small plywood board that has several items glued to it. My attention is immediately riveted to the penny. I adore pennies and collect them. I have at least ten of them at home. I tell him this, but he immediately starts

50

asking about some grown-up thing called "coin collecting," and the conversation breaks down. I devote myself so assiduously to trying to pick off the glue with my fingernails that he takes a penny out of his pocket and gives it to me so that I'll move on to something else.

He produces an ancient metal doll and an ancient metal dog, much larger than the girl. There is a tiny shoe like an elf boot glued to the board and I make several futile attempts to put the foot of the doll into the shoe, but it doesn't seem to fit. She is wearing a similar shoe on her other foot, and I can't determine whether the two shoes are the same size. I put the girl on the dog and say, "This is her horse."

"Oh, is that a horse?"

Is he serious? Does he really not know? He can't possibly be this unfamiliar with his own toys.   "No, it's a dog. She's *pretending* it's a horse."

He observes me with rapt attention. "Where is she going?"

"To her grandmother's house." This is because the red metal dress reminded me of *Little Red Riding Hood.*

"Oh? Do you like to go to your grandmother's house?"

"I don't know. I never go there."

He seems to draw a negative conclusion from this, and I can't quite figure out how to clarify things—how to tell him that Alabama, the mythical land of grandparents and cousins and a vanished dog named Spot, all so vivid in the

51

memories of the rest of my family, is a long way from Tacoma. I can't explain to him that we moved from there when I was six weeks old and have only returned once, before I was two, and a big brown man threw me in the air and caught me, and my uncle Buddy, a doctor, gave me a shot which I famously remembered and remember remembering. This occurred when I felt a pain in my bottom when bumping down the stairs on my rear end a few months after the trip (not yet having mastered the art of walking down steps) and I told my mother, "Uncle Buddy sticked my seat." I remember saying this, but I don't remember the actual shot.

This is all too much for me to explain, so I have to let him assume that my lack of visits to my grandmother's house bespeaks a problem of family discord and some sort of deprivation for me. It was a short time after the Alabama trip that I formed the strong intention to remember the events of my life, since obviously no one else was going to do it, and no one else (except maybe Nancy) seemed to even believe that very young children could remember their thought processes. If only it had occurred to me sooner to fix events in my memory, then maybe I could have made him understand. In any case, I will definitely make it a point not to forget this weird interview.

There is also a tiny hat like an elf hat that I try to place on the doll, but it doesn't seem to fit either. I decide his toys are lousy because they're all from different sets.

He takes a quarter and a nickel and a dime from his pocket and asks me how much money he has in his hand.

"How many, you mean?"

He doesn't quite know how to answer. "Yyyess."

"One, two, three!" I count exultantly. Three is my favorite number.

"How much? How many *pennies'* worth?" he specifies, trying to speak my language.

I lift up the quarter to see if there's a penny hidden underneath. "No pennies!" I say triumphantly, pleased to have seen through the trick.

Soon after he returns me to my mother and sister. "How was it?" Nancy asks. "What did you have to do?"

"It was fun. He gave me a penny."

This causes Mother to flare with an odd mixture of fear and anger. "*Why* did he give you a penny?"

"Because I *wanted* it," I whine. "It's mine. He *gave* it to me." I'm afraid she's going to make me give it back. To my relief she doesn't and we leave.

My further elaboration of events only seems to add to my mother's disquiet: he had offered to let me make a phone call; he tried to play a trick on me with money; he had said something about killing Nancy. And for some strange reason, he didn't know I was a girl. He thought I was a man! My account makes Mama very nervous, but

Nancy laughs. She knows I've gotten it all wrong and she'll get the real story out of me later.

Another strange thing happens when we get home. I am immediately dressed in my pajamas, a vintage pumpkin-colored one-piece with a flap that buttons in the rear, one button of which is always either missing or unbuttoned. This garment, one of my favorite items in the world, was previously worn and loved by my older brother and sister, and was a hand-me-down from Mother's cousin Billy Bryan Middlebrooks. I am told that it's because I'm sick, I have a fever, that I am put into pajamas before supper. The truly strange thing is that I'm allowed to go outside to play *barefoot* even though I'm "sick."

Outside I flaunt my sartorial splendor before a group of surely envious neighborhood kids.

Later I pepper my mother with questions about what was up with the man with the old-fashioned toys. She had gotten a job teaching at the Annie Wright Seminary for Girls, and wished to enroll me in four-year-old kindergarten there, though I was a few months too young to do so. The man had been a "psychologist," whose job it had been to assess whether I was "ma-toor" enough for this—a requirement placed by the headmistress before she would consider early admission.

I wanted to go back to see the strange, shy man, having found his serious manner and age-inappropriate questions oddly flattering, but I was made to understand that this would never, ever happen. I overheard that my mother had been very angry that he had taken me into his office alone without clearing it first with her or even interviewing her, and that she believed him to be inexperienced and uninformed with regard to the developmental level of three-year-olds. It seemed that the evaluation had been scheduled against my father's wishes, which may explain why I was allowed to strut around in my daring, sometimes bottom-baring garb despite supposedly being sick. She may have fed me the sick line in case I blurted something out about having been to the "doctor" before she had a chance to come clean with my father herself.

I also suspect that as a stranger in Yankee land she had fears that the fact that money had changed hands and I had said the doctor had been uncertain as to my gender might be an indicator of sexual abuse, and that she had changed my clothes to check me out. And despite her eagerness to have me enter school she doubtless had misgivings about terminating my babyhood, and may have dressed me up in baby clothes to signal this.

"So what did the psychologist say?" I asked, and finally years later got as full a scoop as I would ever get as to my unusual friend's true opinion of me. My verbal skills were fine, my math skills virtually non-existent, motor skill very immature, and apparently my following-directions and respect-for-authority quotient was sadly not up to snuff. Most likely my disbelief in the need to write a "sir name" had something to do with that.

Despite his reservations I was allowed to enter kindergarten in the fall. There the fact that I was the only kid who still wore white high tops earned me the hated nickname "Baby Shoes," but otherwise it was a pleasant school year, marred only by forced sessions at the dining room table with a hated *Jolly Numbers* workbook. I probably had Mr. Psychologist and his low opinion of my ability to add up change for that.

No one could explain to me his intentions with regard to the doll and the dog and the little hat and shoe. Though I shared my mother's opinion that he knew almost nothing about children my age, it was a fascinating and eye-opening experience, a tiny crash course to prepare me for the world of school.

By the time I was five I had abandoned the memory project entirely, feeling that by then I had amassed sufficient evidence to prove my point—that yes, even very early memory could be retained intentionally. The practice in reconstructing whole conversations came in handy later when, for example, there was an especially stunning therapy session that I wanted to preserve. I also used it several times after visits to Alabama to record a snatch of the cacophony of talk and a few snapshot images of the personalities of the rapidly exploding cast of characters.

Chapter eight

Water and Fishes

But in many ways my memory is worse than most: where I put something twenty seconds ago, the name of a movie someone alluded to in their last sentence, the reason I just walked across the kitchen, and how to perform pretty much any operation on a computer no matter how many times it's been explained—these things elude me.

And just as my own ability to perform an occasional feat of memory has its flawed underbelly, so, too, the happy family, both nuclear and extended, contained madness, murder, dark depression, injustice, alcoholism and deep denial. What I do not intend: a Pollyanna gloss on the truth or pointless, cruel exposure; a dull recitation of begats; or a tedious trudge along any particular timeline. So I claim the right to include vast lacunae: entire family branches missing, decades, places of residence omitted, even my own marriage.

I: I'm in the church nursery sitting at a low table strewn with torn books with a Helper. I follow the tale of *The Little Gingerbread Man* with a morbid fascination. Just why did he feel the need to escape the kindly grandparents? Poor, poor little cookie who so fears drowning that he lets the fox devour him, limb by limb.

My favorite here is *The Little Lost Raindrop*, about a big baby teardrop-looking thing that finds itself separated from all the other water. It searches sorrowfully and finally finds the ocean, which it joins and is then lost, lost yet again in togetherness. This one breaks my heart every time.

II: Mrs. Fisk, my gray-haired babysitter, takes me shopping with Nona, her daughter. Nona has long black hair and a wide, full skirt like a gypsy, but she is no free spirit. She follows behind her mother mournfully, doing as she is told, placing first her own baby, the solemn, bald-headed lump Melita into a stroller, and then me. Even though I'm a walking, talking Big Girl of three, they've brought an extra stroller for the long walk from the bus stop.

I warm to the occasion. A woman and a little girl about age five approach us. "Look, Mama, look! Two babies," she says, in the slow, sing-songy voice of the gullible.

I ham it up. "Wawa," I say, waving my arms. "Fishy! Wawa!"

III: Strangest of all the tales my father reads to me at night is that of the seriously disturbed little boy who wants nothing in the world, not pink ice cream, not a trip to the circus, except to be a fish. What could possibly have befallen this angry, stubborn child to have him pulling at his sister's hand to reach the ocean? Where in the world are their parents? They are by the dark, cold ocean all alone.

After shucking off his red-striped shirt and trousers, he leaps into the waves and is accosted by some scary-looking fish. Then he wises up and goes for ice cream instead. But still. What the heck was wrong with this kid?

IV: It's the 4th of July and I am four. We're on a boat in Puget Sound. Daddy holds me up over the railing so that I, too, can see the jellyfish below. I'm in my magical red pedal-pushers, the ones in which I always envision myself doing something to save the world, and a white print shirt, which he has inadvertently pulled up, exposing my tummy to the wind.

Daddy is such a tease. I have to be careful, careful, of how I choose my words. If I say, "Put me down," he just might throw me over to the jellyfish as a joke. I think and think and at last come up with, "I'm cold."

He puts me down. Safe.

Note: My father had never done anything to warrant such a suspicion.

V: For years my life has been a secret from my parents. Scarcely a word of hope, fear, wish, true interest or excitement ever passes my lips in their presence.

I am seventeen years old and home from college. I spend hours talking on the phone with my friends or writing letters. Mother hounds me, hurt and angry, to talk to her. Few topics seem safe—not guys, not friends, not teachers or other people's parents—she is far too jealous of my connection to anyone else, far too easily horrified and alarmed for this. Any real talk of our relationship would likely send her howling over the edge.

Not poetry: that's way too personal. Not plans: I have none, beyond my next escape. Not sex or cigarettes or books or movies. Not religion. Not politics. Not art.

Finally I hit upon something that seems harmless. We are driving down the precipitous slope of Louden Heights Road in Charleston, and I'm behind the wheel. "I dreamed last night that we were back in Tacoma," I say. Surely that fits the bill: it's personal, a dream; it concerns family history; it hints at nostalgia, a return to former times.

"But it wasn't really our old house. It was a big house, of sort of a nautical design. There was a reflecting pool in the front yard and a pond in the backyard."

Mother clears her throat, ominously. "Well, I never told you this." Already I am sorry that I brought it up. "But when you were two-years-old I dreamed another soul entered your body."

I break out in chills and nearly crash into the guardrail.

"There was a little girl in Tacoma who drowned, in a pond near her home. Her father was a sea captain, I believe. Anyway, I had that dream and then you started having nightmares. You would wake up screaming about water and fishes. And I was terrified, terrified!"

That was it. No elaboration. So, what, I'm a changeling? I have a dual soul?

I seek the division, the transition, inside me. But it has all merged together, seamless as the ocean of my experience. Good thing I started paying attention when I did.

Chapter nine

Toys and Games

Mrs. Fisk lived across the street in the small house also inhabited by her daughter Nona, Nona's formidable husband, Earl Prout, and their two children, Melita and Noweta. Noweta was a year younger than Nancy, and one of our most frequent playmates. I recall her running fearfully across the street with something hidden inside her coat.

"I stoled my doll," she confessed, breathless.

Their strange house had had a whole roomful of toys. What would have been the dining room had aisles of tables on which were displayed a few decades of toys: tiny cash registers, telephones, dolls, cars, stuffed animals. Children were not allowed to touch these things. It was Earl's private collection.

Earl was an electrician, and much to be feared. There was a special amber-colored bar of soap in their bathroom that only he could use. My mother had returned to teaching science and math, and my time in the care of Mrs. Fisk was divided between their house and ours. The soap was always dry when I checked it. It smelled wonderful.

The Prouts bought their bread from a bread truck. The picture of the loaf on the side had pink flowers, and I assumed the bread in the package had the same decoration. I greatly coveted some. Mrs. Fisk once bought me a loaf, but it was just regular white bread. Likewise, when I expressed the wish to eat dandelions, Mrs. Fisk informed me that they were, in fact, edible. We collected dandelion leaves for days, and then they were boiled up into a spinachy mess flavored with vinegar. No yellow flowers.

The Prouts treated me better than their own children, it seemed to me. I remember even Earl patting me gently on the head, and one time he led me on a rare tour through the toy room. On my fourth birthday they presented me with fabulous gifts: an alphabet book, The *Three Little Pigs*, a plastic smock apron for use in finger-painting, and small postcards from Vancouver, Canada bound into a little book.

Only once do I remember misbehaving at their house. I scooped fingerfuls of coconut icing from a cake on the kitchen table. Nona saw it first. "Mama! Mama!" she cried, being unable to deal with the situation herself. Mrs. Fisk then scolded me, but the overriding concern was to hide the evidence from Earl.

I remember Noweta running out of the house to escape Earl with his belt. And Nona coming up to our car in January, 1958 just as we were starting to pull away for our move to Virginia. She had one last gift for us: two elegant handmade dresses for the Kim dolls, a forerunner of Barbie, that Nancy and I had. Nona was crying. We had been her only friends.

Our brown-shingled house on North Elm Street in Tacoma had been in a variegated neighborhood. There were huge, three-story houses inhabited by elderly rich people, or divided into apartments for the working poor. There were middle-class single family homes like ours and the Howes' next door, and ramshackle dwellings devoid of furniture, but littered with broken toys.

My mother had grown up in a small town where children roamed freely from dawn to dusk, when they weren't working. She didn't know about the tiny apartment where I regularly visited a single mother and her two small children or the house where a naked, unsheltered bathtub sat at the top of the stairs. She was also blissfully unaware of the wildness of some of our adventures. By far the best of these had been climbing onto the roof of an apartment building with a group of little kids and dipping our hands into a bucket of warm tar. The evidence from this had been incontrovertible, however.

My classmates at the Annie Wright Seminary for Girls ("cemetery," Mike joked) were from much wealthier families. Mother was teaching there, so we got a big discount on tuition. Nancy also attended briefly, and the school violated its almost iron-clad policy by skipping her from second grade to third. Her much advanced reading ability had been the impetus for this.

My class included the daughter of a senator and another whose father was a newscaster. Fat Carl was feted with birthday parties on a yacht, which we all attended. Likewise Carla (no relation to Carl) had sumptuous birthday parties at their mansion. Said to be the granddaughter of the richest man in Canada, sweet, dull-eyed Carla had envied my ability to learn.

When the newspaper photographer had covered our May Day Festival for the society page, he had selected a photo of me handing a flower to the May Queen to run in the paper. Apparently he had not known that I, in my homemade dress, was of the *hoi polloi*.

In Nancy's class most girls were already boarders. They greatly envied us for getting to live with our parents, and when I had to wait a few hours after the kindergarten half-day to wait for Mama to finish teaching, the lonely boarders vied to help take care of me. I was similarly favored by the cooks, who were pleased by my fondness for asparagus, which was almost daily fare.

Rigmar

Annie Wright employed some displaced Europeans as teachers. Miss Bredis, who was French, was much dreaded as a playground monitor. She demanded total silence, no running, and would line us up facing the wall with our hands up for our infractions of sound and movement.

Rigmar Hornbec, who was Danish, was much loved by all. She had been Nancy's teacher during her brief stint in second grade. It was our great privilege to have her live with us. She moved into my brother's bedroom on the ground floor, for which he had been allowed to choose the colors: a stunning burgundy and chartreuse. Mike moved down to the rollaway bed in the basement, where he had to contend alone with whatever goblins remained behind the cabinet.

Nancy and I would argue over who loved Rigmar the most. The high point of the day was being allowed to select a single M and M from her stash before supper. She taught us how to make woven paper nut cups at Christmas, and it was she who selected the name for my doll, Polenski.

My great aunt Rubye had sent me a dollar for my fifth birthday. With it I bought a sawdust-filled, cloth-covered doll made in Poland, who was wearing a peasant dress and cap. I had picked her out of a bin stuffed with identical dolls. Not wanting to boast about my new acquisition, I had said to Rigmar, "It's not really such a nice doll."

Rigmar almost exploded. I had never seen her angry before. "That doll was probably made by a child your age! You have no idea how fortunate you are, how poor they were and still are! What they saw, what they endured, what happened there!" She caught herself, calmed down and chose the name.

Chastened, I envisioned five-year-olds already smart enough to use a sewing machine. I elevated Polenski to a place of honor in our pantheon of dolls, higher even than my elegant Sue and Valentina, and above Nancy's magical Toni and Nora. Polenski ruled serenely, though you couldn't change her clothes.

It was not until two years later that I first saw pictures of the Holocaust, in a book of *Life Magazine* photos...the piles of naked, starved bodies, many of whom were children. "WHO DID THIS?" I asked, outraged.

My mother and sister explained that once upon a time there had been a bad man named Hitler. But it was clear, from the scope of the carnage, that he had not acted alone. "One person didn't do all this. Who helped him?" I asked.

"The German people."

"What's the matter with them? Are they evil? Are they just horrible, horrible people?"

And then the very sad and even more alarming truth, from my mother. "No. They're really not so different from us."

The very obvious conclusion: "You mean something like this could happen HERE?"

Nancy and Mama hastened to reassure me. No, no, the bad man was dead, and they had had a dictatorship, whereas we had a democracy with checks and balances.

"How did he make people do this?"

"By telling lies about the Jewish people."

"What were the lies?"

"He said they had stolen money, but they hadn't," Nancy simplified.

"They did THIS to CHILDREN because they thought they had stolen MONEY??" Monstrous,

monstrous...I resolved that if a bad man ever took over my country, that I would not fall for his lies, that I would sound the alarm in whatever way I could. I did not for one minute believe that our system of government was so impervious to breach that it could never happen here.

Scrabble Comes to Our House

The Christmas of 1956 was a big one for the Griffin family. I asked for and received a ballerina doll, which was a favored item with my more flush classmates at Annie Wright. In the weeks prior to Christmas I had searched under my parents' bed and found the doll clothes my mother was making for my future Valentina. This confirmed what I had long suspected: there was no Santa Claus. I was pleased to announce this later to Nancy and Mike.

"You're just now figuring that out?" was their response.

But the big excitement was a secret we three children were in on and miraculously managed to keep. Mama was giving Daddy something he really wanted—two things, really—a Scrabble set and a brand new dictionary to replace the tattered, coverless one that they had used for over fifteen years. The cost alone of these two objects was impressive. They each cost ten dollars, and the total of twenty was a large number of dollars for a parental gift in those days. My parents had played the game at a friend's house, and Daddy, always a word lover, had been enthralled.

The socks and underwear he typically received as gifts had never caused much of a stir, but Scrabble, in its burgundy cardboard box, and the new dictionary, with its tan faux leather cover on which his name was embossed in gold, had really lit him up.

The game rapidly outflanked our nightly games of Parcheesi and even Honeymoon Bridge, which I knew Mama and Daddy played after we went to bed. (I had often begged them to leave up the fabulous constructions of cards, like card houses, which I imagined they built at night, but their bridges had been disassembled back into small card stacks every morning.)

Scrabble became a nightly ritual for them.

One Saturday morning Daddy decided it would be educational to teach Nancy and me, then nine and five, to play. Mike, whose severe, undiagnosed learning disability made spelling a torture for him, was allowed to be excused.

Though the rules had been explained, I eagerly searched for the letters of my name on my first rack. I found a close approximation, EMO, which was my nickname then, and played it happily. It was challenged off. Nancy and Daddy said it was a "proper name," even though it was a nickname!

On a following turn I played DETE, which was the name of a character in my favorite book. Mama had paid a quarter at a yard sale for a first edition translation of Johanna Spyri's *Heidi*, which became my most treasured possession. "Dete" had been the name of the bossy governess.

This, too, was challenged off, but Daddy allowed me to replay it as DEET. The name of the insecticide was already in the dictionary by then.

This mollified me somewhat, but I was still fuming over not being allowed to play a "proper name" when Daddy laid down BILL.

"Hey that's *your* name!" I objected. "How come you get to play your name and I couldn't play mine?"

"It's not a proper name."

"I know! Your name is really William! But why do you get to play *your* nickname? You wouldn't let me play mine!"

Nancy injected, "You know, like 'dollar bill'? That's not a proper name. Or a nickname."

This of course made perfect sense, but I was too mad to admit it. The sound of the uproar drew Mama out of the kitchen, and I was banished for being sassy and sent upstairs to take a nap.

Some sixty years later I was vindicated when EMO was finally included in the *Scrabble Dictionary.*

Chapter ten

McLean and Radicalization

In Mclean, Virginia the neighborhoods were more homogenous than ours in Tacoma had been. There were blocks and blocks of cookie-cutter houses inhabited by middle-class, all white families headed by fathers with mostly government jobs. Our house in Tacoma had cost $6,000 in 1953 and sold for $12,000 five years later. By then Sputnik had happened, and government-employed engineers were given a large raise across the board. Our family benefitted, even though Daddy, as a hydrologist, could hardly be expected to help compete in the space race. Our house on Dillon Avenue cost $21,000.

Greer and Gladys M. who lived around the corner were my parents' closest friends in the neighborhood, though they were significantly older. Greer was a CIA agent, and when we had dinner there we were treated to slide shows of their supposed vacations in Europe.

There was much moving in and out of the neighborhood during our five year tenure there. For a time there had been few children my age, so I started a little school for the three to five- year-olds. Gail, Stevie, Barbara and a wild child named Dede Leviticus were my most regular pupils. Dede would wander over from a distant neighborhood far across the creek. In the talent shows we put on in our carport, she always sang a torch song. Barbara was always a "Canadian," by which she meant comedian, and would pull bizarrely at her hair while shaking her head rapidly from side to side. Stevie favored a routine involving a mat of plastic vomit.

Soon, however, there was a large contingent of girls my age and we formed an organization called "The Rotten Peaches Club," the name inspired by items on the founder's kitchen windowsill. We played with plastic horses, put on plays and ate fabulous snacks, and also played a lot outside—kickball, baseball and wild chasing games of boys against the girls.

At Kent Gardens Elementary the gang of transplanted kids was equally divided in our games of war. "Yankee or Rebel?" was the question. "Rebel," was my answer. We played chase and capture in the tiny patch of woods that still remained.

Radicalization

In the summer of 1961, I was nine-years-old. When we got to Alabama for our yearly visit, the first thing I wanted to do was go see my grandmother's cow. The desultory crowd in her small country store was drinking Nehi's, occasionally plunking down a nickel for a cookie from the jar. As a newly arrived visitor, I could have anything I wanted: all the popsicles, candy cigarettes, cokes—even a guide into the woods to find the cow. "Uncle George will take you," my grandmother, whom we called Aunt (pronounced "Ain't") Maude volunteered.

Uncle George was an ancient black man in overalls and a tattered straw hat. He had red, rheumy eyes and spoke in a guttural patois of which I understood almost nothing. The woods were almost impenetrably dense and steaming hot. The quest for the cow proving fruitless, by degrees I came to understand his personal agenda: to bring his wife, Aunt Susie, a surprise. A guest.

A tiny weather-beaten cabin stood in the clearing and a woman in a long flowered dress was beaming welcome at me from the door. She didn't know me from Adam. "Sammye?" was her guess, the name of the girl cousin my age. But Lou Ellen's daughter, all the way from Washington! That was even better. She invited me in.

I had never been inside a black person's house before. The exotica that awaited: a pot of collard greens and fatback boiling on the stove, of which I was invited to partake. I declined, knowing that I was soon expected at Aunt Maude's. A small cork bulletin board on which were thumbtacked pictures cut from magazines and the pink, curly bow from a gift. I was touched and charmed by the welcome and it helped to fuel even further my disbelief in what I had been hearing.

There had been, and were, all through that visit, whispered conversations about the evils of integration, about "outside agitators" being bused in to stir things up. Justice Hugo Black, local boy who hit the big time, was a traitor to his homeland for supporting the desegregation ruling. (I also heard, much later, that he had been in the Klan. Aunt Mildred had read it in the Greensboro paper. One wonders whether his vote had been bought by the fear of this being exposed.)

These things were whispered so that Janie Dee or Arlee or Viola or whoever was cooking, wouldn't overhear. Aunt Maude even went so far as to forbid Janie Dee to watch television while she ironed so she wouldn't watch the demonstrations and get ideas.

Lest Aunt Maude, the sainted matriarch of the family, emerge here as a kind of villain, allow me to remind you that of the nine children she had successfully raised, three of them, boys in need, had been black. It was a strange paradox that despite the very close family bonds that often existed between blacks and whites, the idea of "separate but equal" schools, the prohibition against intermarriage and strong support for states' rights to guard against federal dictates were tenets of belief strongly held by every white person down there I ever knew back then.

We also visited Great Aunt Jenny that summer of '61 in Selma. There were two oscillating fans on the parlor floor, and she served us lemon pound cake and sweet iced tea as she told us, in a shocked tone, the news about her yard boy. "I asked him, 'You wouldn't do like all these demonstrators, would you?' and he answered, 'No ma'am, Miss Jenny.' And do you know the very next day I saw him on television carrying a sign?"

Of course! What did she expect! I secretly exulted for the yard boy.

Aunt Susie died a few days later in their tiny cabin. Their daughter came from Birmingham to pick up Uncle George, and he stopped by the big house to say goodbye. In his Sunday suit and hat, Uncle George walked up on the well porch to take his leave of my grandmother, to thank her for being good to him the last thirty years or so.

"George," said Aunt Maude in her correcting voice, "You know you need to take your hat off when you come up on the porch."

Take your hat off? That was goodbye to a grieving widower? My blood ran cold. I could only come up with one way to register my outrage. I stalked back inside and slammed the screen door shut.

So, Yankee or Rebel?

Rebel, still, but against what? In my secret heart I was becoming a deserter.

Southern Heritage

How long can you talk about Alabama without talking about race? How long can you talk *in* Alabama without somehow alluding to race? The answer to both questions: not long.

Some thirty-seven years later my cousin Abe presented me with a thirty-page printout of all our cousins and forebears on mother's side of the family, most of whom had lived and died within fifty miles of where we sat, over the last two-hundred-and-fifty years. How long can one's people live in a society devoted to maintaining the racial divide between the haves and the have-nots without committing crimes against humanity, both subtle and profound? I can pretty well guarantee that the answer is *not* two-hundred-and-fifty years.

My Alabama heritage...sometimes I wear it like a scarlet A, a readily identifiable badge of shame. At other times it's like a magic cloak allowing me to pass through portals of opinion so sharply different from my own that were I to be detected, my heretical, yankeefied smart ass might be sliced to ribbons.

It's a lot of things, this garment: neatly tailored, from beautiful cloth, whose texture and color I ogle secretly to keep from dozing off in the middle of a recitation of who married whose third cousin's grandma. It's a heavy, hand-crocheted veil, a landrace pig-pink birthday suit, the tartan of a patchwork clan of German, Scotch and Welsh...but, I'll tell you one thing. It is too damn hot.

When we moved to Washington in 1952, first to Walla Walla, then Spokane and then Tacoma, my father almost immediately shed his southern accent and started going by the name Bill.

Perhaps the set of cartoons of him drawn by a coworker, a playful, friendly ribbing depicting the southerner mired in snow while conducting field tests, had a little something to do with this.

My mother's accent, on the other hand, if anything became more pronounced. She sought fellow southerners as companions, whenever possible. In McLean these included Gladys M., from North Carolina, and my fourth grade teacher, Daisy Belle R., from South Carolina.

Fourth and Fifth Grade

At first I hadn't minded being Mrs. R.'s pet, and was flattered to be called up to her desk for private conversations about what the press was meanly reporting about the South.

As the year wore on, however, the gross disparity between how she treated me and treated others became unbearable to all. She would rage at the other children and make them cry, and in the next breath would be delivering a homily on my wonderfulness.

One day in the cafeteria my good friend Leigh Lindjord, the daughter of an Air Force colonel, said to me, "You see what she's doing, how she's treating everyone but you. It's up to you to make her stop."

My request for a private audience was immediately granted. I explained to Mrs. R. that all her yelling at the other kids and making them cry was not going over well, and that praising me at their expense was widely noted and unappreciated. Her only concern, horribly, was whether this was causing any problem for me. I said that it was, that I was starting to lose friends.

She held a class meeting every afternoon. She started that day's meeting by apologizing to the class, saying that she had been unaware of how badly she had treated them, and that she never would have realized it, never would have addressed it, had it not been for that Wonderful Child...

This was too much for Debbie Fairbanks, my friend standing that day at the door as Sergeant at Arms. Seeming almost in a trance, Debbie interjected, "Mrs. R., Emily hates you."

Uproar, pandemonium, meeting adjourned. With two more months left in the school year, I did damage control as best I could. "I hate you as a teacher," I said, "but I like you as a friend."

The next year, fifth grade, was a very creative time for me. I wrote poetry prodigiously and did a few works of art, one of which was a copy of Raphael's Alba Madonna, first in pencil and then in watercolor. I spoiled the effect, however, when I couldn't resist using dots of black magic marker for the pupils in the eyes.

My friend Adrian and I built a fort in the woods. It was the coolest thing. We found an ample supply of old boards, which we stacked log cabin style to form a structure about three feet high. We found the side of an old shed with an opening that had originally been a window, and this became the roof and the entryway. It was a huge disappointment when some boys tore it down.

We were privileged to live in a golden age of play in that neighborhood, riding our bikes around and around the hilly block, fifteen or twenty kids sledding down the hills in the winter. In summer the croquet games in our side yard went on until it was too dark to see.

All of us, my parents, Nancy and Mike and I, had an abundance of friends. And all of that came to a crashing halt when we moved to Charleston, West Virginia in January, 1963.

Chapter eleven

Outcasts

What I had expected in West Virginia was a bucolic setting and maybe something along the lines of a one-room-schoolhouse. What I found instead was Fernbank Elementary, where my sixth grade classmates were not only several months ahead in math and science of where Mr. Bright's class in McLean had been, but vastly more sophisticated than my previous classmates.

My teacher, Mrs. Wright, had been excited to get a new student. Most of the kids had gone there since first grade, and there was very little turnover. This was my fifth elementary school, and in Virginia I had met at least fifteen new classmates every year.

They were distantly polite to me but rarely friendly. No one invited me to their house, no one came over, and even with the few girls who lived near me I couldn't seem to break the wall of silence. The wisecracking bad boys, Max and Randy, who sat in the back of the room with me were happy to include me in their jokes, however, and Melanie Foster, who was in the other sixth grade classroom but came to ours for math and science was brave enough to break rank once she found out I played piano.

Melanie was (and is) a gifted pianist. In the sixth grade talent show her performance of Debussy's *Clair de Lune* was mesmerizing. She would grill me in the lunch line about my favorite composers. Didn't I love Bartok? And Hindemith! I had never heard of them, but was glad of any chance for conversation.

When the school year ended, lacking the thin shield of protection that well-liked Mrs. Wright had provided, it got worse. A crowd of girls, most of whom I'd never met, jeered and threw things at me when I rode my bike down Ravina Road. One day I stopped to ask them what they were so mad about, since I'd only really met one of them, and they attacked me with sticks. I tried to remain silent about the cause of my bruises, not wanting to make it worse, but my mother ferreted a few words out of me about S., the one girl I knew, and went to talk to her mother.

It did get worse. When seventh grade started at John Adams Junior High, I was a total outcast. Having always had friends, having been the president of my last school in Virginia, this was shocking and painful. The boys joined in the mocking. I would stand outside my homeroom door waiting for it to open, but skinny Mrs. Hyman, who miraculously was always eating, was also always late. Caroline Peyton, actress, singer, guitar player, was the only popular kid whom I recall initiating a friendly contact with me that year. She had heard that I wrote, and wondered if I might want to co-write some songs with her. The idea of co-writing with anyone was anathema to me and I knew nothing about song-writing, but I was glad of the overture to friendship, which has survived to this day.

It was at least a year before I found out what had set off the harassment, and eventually I heard it from at least seven sources. It turned out that Mrs. Wright, after meeting me in the principal's office and looking over my old school record, had made the mistake of going to the other sixth grade classroom and gushing about me being brilliant and beautiful or something. "I instantly hated you," the other girls eventually told me. And it had spread.

Mike was already in the Marines, but my mother and sister experienced something similar. Fifteen-year-old Nancy was jeered and ostracized for her bad skin, and became a recluse, venturing out of her room only for meals and to talk with me alone when our parents were out.

When Mother returned to teaching the next fall, she was loudly, constantly mocked by her students. She had taught in at least eight previous schools, and had never experienced anything like it before.

Despite being super depressed and anxious, sick every day on the way to school, I plugged away at forming friendships and began to make a few. The tide of acceptance had turned so quickly that it was frightening.

Some time early in the eighth grade, a crowd of girls knocked at our front door. Their Girl Scout overnight had been rained out, and they were instead having a slumber party across the street. The group included several of my previous tormenters.

I feared they were there to humiliate me in front of my family, but no, they were there because I was so very funny and they wanted me to entertain them. I did, improvising some kind of comedy monologue on the spot.

My mother's harassment continued. Her cruel nickname was "chickenhead," because of her long neck, and there were prank phone calls, boys driving by in cars screaming and throwing things, and almost daily taunting in the hallway.

She became stranger and stranger, more and more set in her ways. Just about the only safe world, the only one worth talking about, was Alabama prior to 1952. She latched ever more strongly onto me, telling me often that a fortune teller had once told her that she would have one child who would stay with her forever and take care of her in her old age—and that was clearly destined to be me.

My father was the only one who for several years stayed above the fray, successful at work, where he was then District Chief of the US Geological Survey office. He had responsible posts at church and enjoyed his nightly reading and Scrabble games. He even wrote a paper, something about "dimensionless rating curves," that was published in the journal, *Geophysical Year*.

Something bad happened at the end, though, about which I can only speculate. He was demoted and sent back to DC in about 1970.

Why I Went to College

I had the dubious honor of being my mother's favorite child, which has its downside, as was clear with Mrs. R. Though older, Nancy was painfully aware of being an afterthought. I could feel Mother's projection trying to beam itself through my skin—the image of her ideal self at three, then again at ten, a young girl perpetually dressed in white performing flawlessly on an ancient Alabama stage. I was to remain these ages forever, that much was clear—or sometimes I was allowed to be forty. In any event, the sexual awakening portion of my experience was intended to be omitted entirely.

It's a tough job, to be a perfect imaginary other person, and I tried as best I could to refuse the role. I committed all manner of teenage crimes, imperfectly concealed but never confessed. I tried to talk to her about the need to let your children go and pointed to a Reader's Digest article as proof, but she reacted as if I'd uttered the most amusing pleasantry. "Oh, no," she said, shaking her head, laughing gaily. "No...no."

The degree to which my mother dominated our entire family system, even (and especially) in the role of Humble Servant was equaled only by her great fragility. It seemed that anything I did or didn't do might kill her.

It occurred to me to try to seek therapy, but I could only come up with this representation: at my age, in my situation, my inner world would just be plundered, my codes given over to the enemy. I figured the only thing I was likely to be cured of was being the only thing I was sure I was: a poet.

So I devoured the few psychology books that came my way, looking for answers or perhaps a silent version of the talking cure. But talk I did with a bevy of nonprofessionals (teachers and friends) in the publications room at school, on the phone, in the commons area—hours and hours with people who kidded me, confronted me and laughed at my jokes and who wouldn't let me get away with being too weird. During sophomore and junior year at George Washington High this service had been rendered especially by Florence and Melanie. But they were graduating.

It was especially hard when my father went out of town on business, and I was left alone with Mother's tears, her mounting horror at the inexorable tide of vulgar modernity, and at my suspected defection to the enemy camp of change. I despaired of ever getting out alive.

A tiny crack of opportunity appeared in November, 1967. Melanie was in our kitchen, and we were both sixteen. She had gone about as far as she could go then in Charleston's music world, having won both the amateur and professional divisions of the West Virginia classical music competition, first with a Saint Saens concerto, and then with Prokofiev. Before the school board slammed the door on such applications, she had asked for and received permission to graduate early.

"Why don't you do that, Emily?" Mother asked brightly, passing by with a stack of folded towels. She didn't mean it for a minute and was well aware of the school board ruling.

But I pretended to believe she was serious. And after all, she had done the same thing, graduating at the tender age of fifteen.

As soon as Melanie left I went upstairs to my parents' room and called a member of the school board. (Melanie had given me the number.) Yes, I knew about the recent ruling by the board, but since permission had already been granted to another member of the Junior Class wouldn't it be only fair to allow me to do the same thing, to graduate early? Yes, I had exhausted all the relevant educational opportunities. Yes, I had my parents' support...My mother was a teacher and she had suggested it! Certainly I would talk to my principal, my guidance counselor and get their advice...oh yes, yes. Thank you. I'll let you know.

When Miss Heiserman, the buck-toothed guidance counselor, had asked me if I wouldn't benefit more from another year at home with my family, my church, I had concentrated hard on trying not to laugh. Gee, it was really a tough decision, sure...but I had talked it over, and it seemed that this was really for the best.

I pulled it off, and then presented my parents with the done deal. My father was proud, my mother shocked and horrified. "Hey, I'm only

89

following in your footsteps, doing what you told me! Surely that's okay!" I had her then.

Why Vanderbilt? Because they had a policy of accepting high school juniors and the fact that it was below the Mason-Dixon line made it palatable to my parents.

Chapter twelve

Meeting Margie, and Four Bills

The summer of 1969 was the last time I ever spent more than a week at my parents' house, I believe. Mike, then in the Coast Guard and stationed in the Philippines, had gotten married in the town of Itbud to a local, Margarita Pajudpud. They were returning to the states but he was being sent out again immediately, and there would be nowhere for Margie to go but to our house in Charleston.

Uncertain about how our parents might receive a brown-skinned daughter-in-law, he wrote to me at Vanderbilt to ask if I would stay in Charleston for the summer. He wanted me to help look after Margie and run interference, if necessary. I agreed.

Margie was about six months pregnant when she got there, and spoke very little English. She also had hardly any clothes. I gave her a smock dress I had made, light flowered cotton, and I can't remember her ever wearing anything but this and the orange dress with the bow in front she had been wearing when she arrived. I am sure, however, that my mother bought her other clothes.

She shuffled mournfully from room to room, trying to be of help. When given or shown almost anything she would say, "Very nice," with a sad chuckle. She referred to my brother then and always as "she."

On the hibachi grill outside she cooked a Filipino favorite: pork first marinated in 7-Up and then deliciously spiced.

My niece Mary Jane Griffin was born that November in Miami. My parents were, in fact, thrilled to be the grandparents of the "little China doll," as she was called when she made her debut in Arlington, Alabama six years later at Aunt Maude's funeral.

Mike asked a similar favor of me once more. In 1973 they were stationed in Honolulu, and Margie was pregnant with their second child. Particularly since he didn't know when he would be called out to sea, he asked if I would come to take care of three-year-old Mary Jane and drive Margie to the hospital, if need be. I spent about six weeks there.

William Phillip was born in October, and was at first called Phillip. However, as a toddler, after spending time with my father, he changed his name. "Me Bill," he had asserted, and Bill he remained. Michelle followed in August, 1975.

After I got divorced in 1995, my parents came to visit me in Nashville for the last time. Mother was very incapacitated by arthritis, and my father was so blind he could barely see the Scrabble board at all. It was a good visit. That Sunday I took them to the small Methodist Church down the street. One thing stands out. As one of the last surviving men of his generation in

Arlington, where they had retired, my father had much missed the company of other men. For some reason, I had let him out of the car first, and followed a few moments later with Mother. He had struck up a conversation with the ushers outside the door, and was standing there happily amongst his own kind—men all about the same age, all in suits, and all, oddly, with the same first name. "There are four Bills!" he said in excitement, when Mother and I joined him.

About ten days later he died from a heart attack after another happy visit with my sister, her husband Dan Brown, and their children Joe and Emily. And once again there were four Bills: my father in the coffin, and three of the pallbearers; Bill Griffin, Bill Nettles and Bill Barfield, the son of his long dead sister Mary Belle.

Chapter thirteen

The House

So, where's home? A common question, but a tough one. Montgomery, where I was born but lived for only six weeks? Tacoma, the first home I remember? McLean, because I loved it so much, or maybe Nashville where I have lived nearly continuously since the fall of 1968? Never Charleston, though it was there I met my closest lifelong friends.

In dreams, the archetypal home, my true north were it not so far south, is a house I never lived in. The following is mostly drawn from a chapter I wrote for some book about twenty years ago. Despite my stern injunction not to do so, Aunt Mildred had injected her own slant without checking with me first before giving chapter to the publisher. I've updated and amended this a bit.

Just a few hundred yards past the historical Arlington Methodist Church, on the other side of Wilcox County Road 32, stands a two-story Greek Revival style white house that bears silent testimony to the history of this once thriving town. Once home to no less than seven doctors, Arlington's last gas pumps shut down nearly four decades ago when the Arlington Mercantile closed. An incongruously modern telephone company building is now the town's only business establishment since Dr. Buddy Nettles, its founder, closed his doctor's office.

The house that has borne witness to over 180 years of trade and travel here could now be called the Nettles-Griffin-Brown home. Lou Ellen Nettles Griffin (known in this region as "Miss Lou Ellen") purchased the house, two tenant houses, a barn and about ten acres for the princely sum of $1,000 back in 1938, inflation having driven up the price by $270 since it had last changed hands in 1909.

An enterprising young teacher, Miss Lou Ellen had been sufficiently impressed by the ravages of the Depression to see the need for some serious permanency planning for her family. In particular, she wanted to be sure that her mother, Janie Maude Rikard Nettles, would always have a home. It was expected that Miss Maude would substantially outlive her husband, Samuel Cornelius Nettles, Sr. who was thirteen years her senior. Miss Maude and Mr. Neil had run a busy country store in the small white building to the left of the house, which for about twenty years after that served as the local post office. Now that commerce has died down, one can park here with impunity.

The front yard is entered through a white picket fence, and one walks down a path of the original brick, fired in a kiln on the property when the house was built in about 1838. A magnolia tree to the left is of more recent vintage: it was planted in 1891. A companion tree to the right at first appears to be a match, but on closer inspection proves to be a bay tree—a handyman's error sometime around the turn of the twentieth century.

One steps up onto a wide front porch where rockers and gliders cluster in companionable groups. The double front door, which is unlocked by the skillful juggling of a five-inch-long iron key, is made of the original heart pine. Though the house was continually occupied until 2004, the fact that the exterior once went unpainted for fifty-six years says something about the durability of this native wood.

The wide front hall once stood open at both ends, with a view to maximizing whatever breezes blew on sultry summer nights. An ingenious design drew currents of cool air up from the bottom of the house and out crescent-shaped ventilation panels in the attic. An air shaft was located near the staircase.

The staircase was reversed sometime after the original construction so that it no longer faces the front door. The story goes that one of the original owners felt the need to keep a closer eye on the comings and goings of his offspring, so he put the bottom of the staircase across from his bedroom, which is now a formal dining room. The gender of the offending children is in question, but the fact that the "daughters' room" was built with no egress to the hall attests to a concern about elopement.

In pre-Civil War days what is now the family room was called a "dog trot," and opened into the "winter dining room," which is now the kitchen. The "summer dining room," to the right, is now a bedroom and bath.

The house boasts many of the original doors, which stick and swing open at whim. Wide plank floorboards peek out from under area rugs. Wavy glass windows in the double doors to the family room are etched with the names of ancient swains of the Dumas and Kimbrough families, who were said to want to prove for themselves the hardness of a diamond ring.

A more intriguing legend has to do with hidden treasure. Alarmed by reports of approaching Union soldiers, the original owner Joel Dumas buried gold amassed from selling crops and livestock, but wrapped the silver in a "croker sack" and dropped it down the well.

It amused the locals to watch the Union soldiers quench their thirst, oblivious to the treasure below. When the army departed, the bag of silver was hauled up with grappling hooks.

The gold met with a different fate, however. In 1838 the builder of the house had lost his entire profit from the job by making the mistake to sit down to a celebratory game of poker with Joel Dumas. So too, Joel Dumas was unable to leave his profits to his heirs. He suffered a stroke and died before revealing the hiding place of the gold.

Generations of treasure seekers have combed the grounds with metal detectors and peered between the boards of the mysterious double walls upstairs, to no avail. An old black man known as Uncle Alex Robinson gave Lou Ellen this cryptic clue when she was a young girl: Joel Dumas had jumped up from his sickbed with the bag of money, and buried it "in a line with the big pine tree." However, as a mathematician, Lou Ellen was sadly aware that an infinite number of lines can radiate from any point. Even the location of "the big pine tree" is no longer known.

To return to what can be known: two of the original outside chimneys still stand, while two of the others have been rebuilt. One of the two original wells is still functional. After ownership passed to Nancy and Dan Brown in 2004, Dan leveled the house by placing numerous jacks underneath and added corrugated tin ceilings in the kitchen and back room.

The table that Neil Nettles built is still in the kitchen. Other furnishings have come down through Maude Nettles and her sisters: a platform rocker dating from 1911, a high double bed with a large headboard, marble-topped dressers and tables and spacious wardrobes. The Griffins added a country French table that seats fourteen, and several chests and cabinets for linen and china. A hand-cranked telephone in the hallway was in use until about 1958.

Deeds record the names of previous owners: Dumas, Threadgill, DeVan, Dumas, and in 1909 Dilger. Lou Ellen purchased the house from an impoverished widow, Benie DeVan Dilger, who sealed the bargain informally by making an exquisite hand-crocheted tablecloth for the young woman's hope chest. "Miss Benie had a tragic life," explained Lou Ellen to her son-in-law Dan

Brown, from Michigan. "She married a Yankee." Indeed, Mr. Dilger had been the son of a Union soldier, a turn of events that might have had Master Dumas turning in his grave.

For more than 80 years now, Nettles, Griffin, Cook, Lavender, Brown, Lizotte and Serna children, grandchildren, great-grandchildren—and cousins, aunts, uncles, second cousins and all the permutations thereof, have found in the hospitality of the old house in Arlington a portion of their own personal history. For each it remains a part, throughout all their far-flung travels, of what it means to have a family home.

Chapter fourteen

The Whole Keyboard

Having set the stage more clearly, I will now populate it with a fairly sizable portion of the cast. The events here described were not, I assure you, held freakishly forever in memory, but recorded shortly after their occurrence in 2002. Since we have arrived in the present century, albeit by a somewhat circuitous route, I will now employ primarily the present tense. It just works better that way.

Setting Out and Catching Up

I am going to Arlington to put on a party for my mother's eighty-eighth birthday, trying to remember all the things I need to gather and do first. Among the things I so frequently forget: hairdryer, toothbrush, underwear, socks and lipstick. The special things include Mother's present. It's a wooden trivet/cutting board, the edge of one spiral-cut side of which lifts, ingeniously, to form a basket. It was made in Scottsboro, Kentucky and carved from a single piece of wood, so the man said. I'm taking mixed nuts for the party and three summer sausages, one for Mother and one for each of her helpers, Shirley and Lyda. Shirley almost always presents me with Conecuh Sausage when I visit, which is named for the county of my father's birth.

What I nearly forget to do is to fax a treatment plan for a client to United Behavioral Health. C. is just so cool, so functional, that I fear I haven't made her sound sick enough to warrant further treatment, despite her history of having been forced as a small child to witness prolonged episodes of Ku Klux Klan torture and murder, and her repeated rape by a multitude of family members. If I let myself think about it I'll start wanting to shoot people, so I don't.

Another thing that's really getting my goat as I set out, besides, as always, torture, is the thought of what my cousin Johnny has been going through related to his divorce. (Out of concern for both courtesy and liability, this portion is intentionally expurgated.)

Listening to a CD in which the clear, tiny voices of pygmies warble in a lush electronic mix, I pull up behind a battered Impala whose back window is covered with adhesive letters of different sizes. The effect is of a demented ransom note: "REAL MEN LOVE JESUS" "HOLY INSURANCE." From the looks of the sprung trunk, this guy needs some.

Near Safford the sky turns tornado black and rain pelts down. A black man without an umbrella is walking on the side of the highway. I consider backing up to offer him a ride, but press on.

It's dry at Mother's house. I have taken care to arrive an hour ahead of schedule, knowing the anxiety that being even a few minutes past ETA can cause. Shirley answers the door and I hug her, then go to Mother's chair to kiss her hello. Shirley gives me the kitchen tour: there's a bowl of barbecued chicken, another of potato salad, and baked beans in the refrigerator. In the freezer there are pork chops and the birthday cake from Walmart.

Mother catches me up on current events: Lyda's nephew, Michael, has come to live with them and he'll be in Jullian's class. (Note: Jullian is Mother's black surrogate grandchild. Now ten, he has lived in this house twelve hours a day since he was four.) They say Michael is hyperactive, but Mother thinks he's cute. Wasn't that strange about Mildred? A sewing needle embedded in the top of her foot! They thought it had been there for years. Rose Ellen came for a visit, but she only brought six of the children. (Note: Rose Ellen is Mother's niece.)

We decide on three o'clock Sunday for the birthday party, and I go to the kitchen to call Aunt Rose Mary (wife of Buddy, mother of Rose Ellen) to invite her. She fills me in on more about Rose Ellen's visit: three of the children had been sick and vomiting the whole time, and one of the twins had broken Susan's nose, banging her with his head when they were running to catch a ball.

I fix Mother's supper in the microwave, then pull one of the chairs next to the recliner to cut her fingernails while she tells stories. At 8:30 I lift her out of the chair and plop her in the wheelchair. The next transfer is more difficult:

hoisting her out of the wheelchair, I nearly drop her on the floor before maneuvering her onto the mattress, where I begin the complicated process of disrobing, changing, bathing. She talks the whole time: Miss Lena Dixon...Grandma...the principal in Manassas. When I turn the light off she instantly falls asleep.

I get up at 6 a.m. and bring her a washcloth and her teeth. I crank up the bed to make it easier to tend to her. For breakfast she chooses grapefruit sections, a piece of cheese toast and half a cup of black coffee, which prompts her story about drinking coffee for the first time at age five at a hotel in Selma with her grandfather and her brother Sam. She selects her outfit: the white pleated skirt that I gave her and the pink knit top that Lyda gave her. An abalone necklace and earrings that I bought her in the Atlanta Underground completes the ensemble.

I call Aunt Mildred. "Why don't you come over and play Scrabble with us? Would you rather come for dinner (note: this is lunch) or supper?"

She chooses dinner.

"Is 11:30 OK?"

"That's when I eat."

Mildred's Visit

I dig some frozen squash out of the freezer and chill some baby shrimp. Miss Mendy Evans shows up bearing her usual Saturday gift—a plate of apple turnovers and homemade divinity. I escort her up the ramp.

"Doll Baby Wright died," she tells us.

"I surely am sorry, but I'm glad his suffering is over."

"The service is tomorrow in Pine Hill."

Mendy leaves, and Mildred, Mother's eighty-three-year-old sister, arrives.

"You're walking better since they got that needle out of your foot," I compliment her.

"Did you know Doll Baby Wright died?" She's disappointed that we already know.

I boil the squash, then fry it up with bacon, onions and bell pepper. I cook some spinach with lemon pepper and make a shrimp salad, which I arrange on lettuce leaves in Grandma Griffin's potato salad bowl. I bring out rolls, sliced tomatoes, and some of Shirley's potato salad. Mildred watches intently. She has always envied mother for having daughters.

"Maggie Mae says she can't come help me on weekends anymore," she laments. "I don't know what I'm going to do. She had that foot surgery, but she still can't walk right."

"Maybe the same person that stuck a needle in your foot stuck one in hers," I speculate as I slip the bib over Mother's head.

"You need a haircut," Mildred says to me.

"I know."

"Crum needs a haircut, too, but he says all the guitar players have long hair." (Note: Crum is Mildred's grandson.)

"He's just saying that to make you mad."

"He's saying it to make his daddy mad." Mildred takes a roll and makes herself a shrimp

105

salad sandwich. "He did real well at that camp in California. He got the prize for being the most outgoing and another for having the most unusual name."

There had been some debate over whether it was really all right for Crum to accept his uncle Bragg's invitation to attend the John Birch camp for children. After defying his parents to marry a Colombian Catholic, my cousin Bragg (now Dan) had inexplicably (to me) moved to the right of even Mildred and Dan's conservative wing. But what harm could it do to study the Constitution? "Crum made a 24 on the test going in, and a 64 at the end," Mildred says. "The constitution is hard to learn."

Mildred suspects, though I try to stay mum, that my social and political views may differ from those of the rest of the family. She is always trying to explain the Old South to me. "We were poor as Job's turkey, but colored people loved us." She begins to reminisce about Nervy, who worked for them when she was a child. I pass the potato salad.

"She had a twin named Ervy," Mother says. "Their mother was our laundress." (This calls to mind an image of watching the laundry procedure once when I was four. A huge cauldron hung over a fire in the side yard, and the white things were boiled with lye, stirred with a giant wooden paddle.) "When their sister Lizzie got married, they asked Mama to make the dress."

"She made the cake, too. I went to that wedding. Why didn't you go, Lou Ellen? Were you too old?"

"I was ten. I don't know why Mama wouldn't let me go. There was Ervy and Nervy, and Lizzie and Kizzie. There was an older boy, too. What was his name?"

"General Lee," supplies Mildred.

"General Lee! Isn't that an unusual name for a black child?" I ask.

"Shoot, no! My UPS man is named General Lee. His Granddaddy was named General Lee. General Robert E. Lee," Mildred replies.

The story of the three young black men my grandparents raised has always interested me, and I take this opportunity to ferret out more of the facts. "How old was Tony when he came to live with y'all?"

Mother takes this one. "About twelve. Tony Jane Hannah. His middle name was Jane."

"Mama made him go to school," says Mildred. "I'd walk past Buddy's room, and Buddy would be on one side of the fireplace studying, and Tony would be on the other. One time they had a fuss."

"And Mama went in to see what it was about," Mother continues. I butter her roll. "Tony said Buddy had promised him half the money if he won the prize for his essay, but he wouldn't give it to him. What is this? Turnip greens?" Mother asks.

"It's spinach. What was the essay on?"

"Farming. Buddy had asked Tony for the information, and then he won. Mama told Buddy he had to give it to him if he promised," Mildred says.

When Tony had gone for a visit to his biological family he had been accorded the privilege of naming his new baby sister. "And he named her 'Miss Lou Ellen'," Mother says, proudly.

"Where is Miss Lou Ellen?" Mildred asks.

"Birmingham, they told me. I hear she's no good." Mother shakes her head.

"I know you would have wished better for your namesake," I sympathize.

"Tony came to see us one time in Tacoma when he was in the Army," says Mother. I gave him some stationery to write to us on, but he never did."

"He wrote to Mama and Daddy all the time!" Mildred reaches for another slice of tomato. "He came back when he got out of the Army. He asked Daddy for a job. Daddy said, 'Tony, you're grown now! You have to make your own living!'"

"So he went to Mobile and got a job on a shrimp boat," Mother says, raising a quivering spoonful of squash.

"And he drowned. It was real sad. He couldn't swim. Daddy cried and cried," Mildred finishes.

Dessert is the frozen lemon bisque that Nancy made when she visited last week. I mix Mother's pills with applesauce to help her swallow, and feed them to her a spoonful at a time.

Once Mildred has risen from the table and heaved herself in to a recliner, I hate to make her get up. So I set the card table up in front of her and leave Mother in the wheelchair instead of putting her back in her own recliner. The ancient cotton bag that holds the Scrabble tiles is leaking letters from the side and bottom, and I pin it shut with a safety pin, resolving to sew it up later. I have my usual luck, playing all seven tiles twice in succession, first with RENDERS and then with GRAFTERS. Mildred plays RITZ horizontally, and then Mother plays it vertically. After winning the third game in a row I serve them a consolation prize of summer sausage and Ritz crackers, with juice glasses of coke.

"Emily Jane is just too good."

"She's another Shirley. That's how Shirley does me," Mother says.

Mother is nodding off in the fourth game, and Mildred proposes a nap. I offer her the front bedroom, but she says that if she takes her shoes off she'll never get them back on again. Instead she stretches out in the chair.

I put Mother to bed and then go to the middle bedroom to read. About twenty minutes later they are both wide awake again.

We decide to let Mother go ahead and open her presents, since she has firmly instructed the party guests not to bring any gifts. The bag from Shirley holds a ceramic butter dish and some

Imari dusting powder. My sister left a package containing a foot-care kit and some cotton gloves (Mother has the sensation, always, of something sticky and gritty on her hands), and Mildred has brought her a bath towel. The bag from Lyda contains a paperback Webster's dictionary. Mother says it's because her own dictionaries are too big and heavy for her to use, and she's always asking to borrow Lyda's.

She is charmed by the wooden basket-board from Kentucky I have brought her.

"We'll have to show that to Mack," says Mildred. "He has a man in Destin who can make anything out of wood." She examines the label. "I hear there are white people in Kentucky as poor as our colored people here in Wilcox County," she says, wonderingly.

"I'm sure that's true," I say.

Before supper we reconvene for a final game of Scrabble, which Mother wins. This pleases both of the sisters.

I pull out leftovers and make us each a plate. Mildred thinks I should invite Miss Mendy to the party, even though she's not family, and says that of her household, her son Abe and his three children are coming, but Helen has to go to Coy to give a talk to a prayer group. They'll bring the exchange student from Switzerland, who just arrived a week ago. "He's six-foot-five, so they're making him play football, but they say he just stands around and looks confused. He knows all about Walmart, though. He knew it was one of the top companies."

Soon after Mildred leaves I put Mother back to bed. I have just found a needle to sew up the Scrabble bag when the phone rings. It's Sammye, the cousin closest to me in age.

Sammye and Them

"Stephanie is another Alpha Gam!" she says. "I just got her settled at Auburn this week. Her roommate is real cute. She looks just like Julia Roberts, and she's from Stone Mountain, Georgia. She pledged Alpha Gam, too."

I have never shared Sammye's social proclivities, but I like her anyway. "That's wonderful."

"It really is. Are Nancy and Dan there with y'all, too?"

"Nancy was here last week, but she went back on Tuesday. It's just the two of us."

"The way Mama was talking, it sounded like half the country was there. What are y'all doing tomorrow?"

"We're having the birthday party at three. Can you come?"

"I don't know. Forrester is out of town and I'm here at Mama's. I have to get ready for school on Monday, and that would put us back kind of late."

"Then why don't you come eat dinner with us? Say around 11:30? How long does it take to get here from Monroeville?"

Mother calls from the next room. "Tell Sammye to bring that picture of Mildred and Jane and all of them standing beside my bed when I was so sick." She heard me say "Monroeville."

Sammye is clearly tempted. "There's nothing like calling up and inviting yourself to dinner. We could leave here around 10:00...We're not GOING to church!" I hear her yell at her mother in the background. "They'll never notice we're not there! What do you want me to bring? Are you sure it's all right?"

"Otherwise we'd just be sitting around waiting for 3:00. What have you got?"

"Chicken salad."

"Sure, bring that. I'll make some pork chops."

When we hang up I call Aunt Rose Mary and ask her if she wants to join us.

"What should I bring?"

"What have you got?"

"I could make that congealed salad with peaches and buttermilk."

"That would be great. I was thinking we needed a congealed salad."

I check the kitchen for supplies and can't find any rice or potatoes. It also seems to me that we need some flowers and some decent rolls, so I take the cordless phone into Mother's room and put it by her pillow. I tell her I'm going to Walmart.

On the twenty mile drive to Thomasville I see two dead deer by the side of the road, and a cluster of police around a stopped car near

Kimbrough. Black women with young children throng the aisles of Walmart. I buy rice, potatoes, Sister Schubert rolls, some apricot-pineapple jam, a jar of Aunt Nellie's corn relish and a beautiful bouquet of red roses and daisies.

I get back around 9:30 and begin to polish silver. Mother and Shirley are hosting the Circle Meeting on Wednesday, and Mother wants to serve fondue in the silver chafing dish. Polishing silver is the one task at which Shirley draws the line: she says it hurts her hand. The chafing dish is a monstrous, four-part affair, but once I've finished, I can't stop. I polish three nut dishes, two silver vegetable bowls, the bread tray and a few pieces of flatware.

I open the doors to the dining room and living room, hoping to cool them off by running the window unit air conditioner in the family room all night. I put the lace cloth on the long table, and set the blue glass plates at the end where I'll serve the cake. I put a napkin, salad fork and spoon at each of the twelve places.

Then I set the table in the family room for five, using Mother's wedding china and silver, and the Austrian crystal. I get out all the serving pieces and slice the lemon while boiling the water to make another pitcher of tea. There's a Mrs. Smith's Apple Pie in the freezer that I decide to bake in the morning. I finally get the Scrabble bag sewn up.

I wake up at six a.m. from a dream in which Mother has climbed the rails and walked to the bathroom. In real life she asks for orange juice, coffee and one of Mendy's apple tarts for breakfast. I preheat the oven for the pie and get her cleaned up. What she has selected to wear for the occasion is the aqua nylon dress she last wore for her Golden Wedding Anniversary. A nightmare. It requires a slip. Yet somehow we achieve the miracle of dressing, and the transfer from bed to the wheelchair, the wheelchair to the recliner. I put on her pearls and earrings and fix her hair, and pile her Sunday School books and Bible on her lap before going off to wash my hair, get dressed, run a load of laundry, vacuum and marinate the pork chops.

My brother calls from Nevada, then my sister and her family call from Colorado. Mother uses the phone by her chair, and I talk on the one in the kitchen. It's the first time I've talked to my niece Emily Kate since she got back from Ecuador. "How did your kids like those school supplies Clint brought them?" I ask.

"Oh, they loved them! The kids were all excited, the teachers were all excited."

Mother is shocked. This is the first she's heard about Emily's male friend visiting her in Ecuador. "How long did he stay?"

"Two weeks."

Nancy gets on the line and I'm just beginning to describe our social engagements when I see a group of people trooping into the family room. This wasn't preaching Sunday, so church got out at 11:00. "Listen, I'll talk to you later. I want to see who all these people are."

It's Jean Ratcliff Creswell, bringing an arrangement of flowers from her garden: zinnias, roses, and a beautiful pink lily. With her are her two teenage daughters and a tall, slender girl wearing lowcut bell-bottoms that reveal about five inches of midriff. This is Nathalie, the new exchange student from Brazil. "That's what she wore to church!" Jean whispers to me, mortified.

I sit down next to Mother and the girls cluster around. Nathalie has been a model in Brasilia, it seems. "Do you play the piano?" Mother asks her, apropos of nothing.

She does.

We begin to tell stories, starting with one that is a favorite with the Spanish-speaking members of our extended family. While in Mexico City to visit some former neighbors, Mother had somehow been alone in their house and made the mistake of answering the phone. Finding herself unable to understand the person on the other end, she had screamed in confusion, "Me no speak English!"

Nathalie smiles politely, not quite getting it.

"I should have said, 'Me no speak Spanish,'" Mother explains.

We talk about what classes the girls will take, and driving. Jennifer and Ann don't yet drive, and Nathalie tells us that you have to be eighteen in Brazil to have a license, but she has been driving some since she was eight.

A home girl! Mother tells about learning to drive a model T when she was ten, and I tell about how, one summer when we visited here, my

115

uncle Dan had been so concerned about my backwardness (I was eleven-years-old and still didn't know how to drive) that he had taught me to drive a Model A.

I tell Jean that Aunt Frances and Sammye are coming, and she decides to stay until they get here. "Your mother's old piano teacher will be here shortly," I explain to her daughters.

Rose Mary comes in with the buttermilk peach salad, and Frances and Sammye follow moments later. Aunt Frances (the widow of Uncle Sam) is resplendent in a royal blue dress.

"I turned ninety-one-years old in July," she announces to the company at large.

"And I was *glad*, too," says Sammye. "I was so tired of hearing about her being ninety-years-old. I'm having a midlife crisis. I've decided to go blonde again," she says brightly to Jean.

"Sammye will be fifty-years-old this year," says Frances.

"How did that happen?" I inquire. "You used to be older than I was."

"I'll be fifty-two in January," Sammye claims. "Mama still doesn't believe I know I how old I am."

I go in to turn on the water for the rice as Jean and her entourage say their goodbyes. Sammye has brought a fuchsia-colored gloxinia, which I put on the marble coffee table in the living room. I stir-fry the vegetables, pop the rolls in the oven and arrange squares of Rose Mary's salad on lettuce leaves on a glass plate. Sammye finishes putting the food in serving dishes (ignoring the newly polished silver bowls!) while I go to haul Mother to the table.

This time I have taken the liberty of assigning seats. I ask Rose Mary to sit in the back corner, since she's one of the young ones who can still get in and out, and place Frances in a more accessible chair at the end. Mother has one side of the table to herself, and I've put Sammye between her mother and Rose Mary, where she can get up to help clear and serve. I'm at the end opposite Frances, with the vase of Walmart flowers in between us. I ask Sammye to say the blessing.

Aunt Frances is still with it in a lot of ways. She still drives a car and teaches piano to twenty students. But for the last ten years or so she hasn't been exactly clear on who I am. Whatever briefing she may have received on the way hasn't done the trick. Peering at me from the other side of the flowers, she tries to solve the mystery. "Where do you live?" she asks, cagily.

My answer has been the same for about thirty years. "Nashville, Tennessee."

"I THOUGHT you sounded like a Yankee," she says, triumphantly.

"Mama, Tennessee's not a Yankee state," Sammye scolds.

Frances is undeterred. "My next door neighbor is a Yankee," she says. "I said something to her about it, and would you believe it? She said she was PROUD to be a Yankee."

I butter Mother's roll and cut up her pork chop. Her bib exactly matches her dress. Everyone exclaims about the food.

"I had no idea you knew how to put on a dinner," Sammye says to me.

Rose Mary drops corn relish on her dress, which upsets her since it means she'll have to go home and change before Doll Baby Wright's funeral.

Frances tells about an adult student of hers who has only been taking piano for six months but can already play for church.

"Did you know Fran was moving her jewelry store?" Mother asks.

Of course they do! Fran is Frances's oldest grandchild.

The phone rings. It's my cousin Bill, calling from Florida. "What are y'all doing?"

"Your mother and sister are sitting here eating with us."

"You're kidding! Let me speak to Aunt Lou Ellen."

Bill's birthday is August 19th, the day after Mother's, so it's easy for him to remember her birthday. He'll turn sixty. I bring the phone to her, and they exchange felicitations. She hands the phone back to me.

"Your mother says she talked to you yesterday, so she won't talk to you right now," I say to Bill and click it off.

Sammye and I have just cleared off the plates and food when my cousin Johnny come in. "Are you hungry?" I ask.

"Starving."

"Hey, Johnny, thanks for buying all those trucks. We really appreciate it. Do you need any

118

more?" Sammye asks. (Note: Johnny runs the telephone company founded by his father, and Sammye's husband, Forrester, has something to do with John Deere products.)

I fix a plate for Johnny. Rose Mary cedes her spot to her son, since she has to go home to change clothes.

I tell them about going to see "Cheval," the Cirque du Soleil horse and rider show. "There was a little four-year-old girl with us, and I kept thinking she was getting the wrong idea, that she was probably thinking that normal people could dance around on the backs of horses. Then at intermission I was talking to her mother and her aunt, and they were saying how they missed doing stuff like that, standing on their heads and doing human pyramids on the backs of horses."

"Wow!" say Sammye and Johnny.

"It turns out that they had been trained as trick riders when their father was a diplomat in Chile."

Johnny considers whether this show would be an appropriate entertainment for his children. "Were there clowns? Allie is scared to death of clowns."

"Like Kramer. There were just two, but they weren't wearing clown suits."

"Then maybe it would be okay."

I invite him to come up some weekend with the children.

We're just finishing up our apple pie and ice cream when Rose Mary honks for Johnny to come take her to the funeral.

119

"We probably should get going pretty soon, too," says Sammye.

"Don't you want to stay and wash these dishes?" I ask her.

She does, thank God.

Sammye is like Nancy: she'd much rather clean up than cook. The china and the hollow-handled knives can't go in the dishwasher, so Sammye washes while I dry and put things away.

"What have you been doing with yourself lately?" she asks.

I tell her I've been writing: non-fiction, for several years, but more recently, fiction. I tell her about a friend in New York giving me character prompts and me cranking out short stories.

"I've always wanted to write about this family," she says. "You know, growing up here in Arlington, I had a fairy tale life. And I couldn't wait for you and Nancy to get here every summer."

"That's what amazed us," I say. We knew you had a fairy tale life. You were like this princess. We were shocked to find out how much you counted on us coming."

"All that spending the night and giggling. Daddy couldn't understand it. Girl stuff, you know. He thought we were just silly."

She tells me she really wants to read what I've been writing. I'm non-committal on that score.

We talk about the classes she is teaching at the private school in Monroeville—music, drama, P.E., and my Pilates class. We commiserate about elder care. She's incensed about the medical care her father-in-law has been receiving.

"He had this doctor, this Boston Jew—not that there's anything wrong with Jews—who didn't believe that anyone else knew anything. And I finally just ordered him to put Mr. Long back on the Serequel. The nurses couldn't believe I got him to do it."

I tell the convoluted story about how a series of medication reactions led to Mother's present inability to walk.

"Mama won't see a doctor or take any medicine."

"That's probably why she's doing so well," I assure her.

There's the rumble of thunder and a flash of lightning. Her mother is terrified of storms and won't go anywhere until it clears up. I tell her about my cousin Jake on my father's side being struck by lightning—twice!

The kitchen is now clean, and we go back to the family room, where Mother and Frances are stretched out on neighboring recliners. Frances tells us she had gone into the living room to try out the piano. "It can still hold a tune," she says. We hadn't heard a thing in the kitchen. She and Sammye argue about a recent storm.

"Sometimes I call her 'Mama,'" Frances confesses.

"Why? Because Sammye's so bossy?" I suggest.

"I wasn't going to say that," Frances giggles.

The rain slows to a patter. Sammye goes to pull up the car, and I get an umbrella to walk Frances down the ramp. It's a good thing: she just got her hair done. We say goodbye.

The Actual Birthday Party

I put the nuts and peppermints in the bowls and set up some fans in a vain attempt to circulate some cool air into the dining room and living room. I get out the glasses for the pink lemonade, and the silver sipping straws that Mother wants us to use. I lift the cake out of the freezer. It's white with yellow roses. "Have a Great 88!" it says.

Around 3:00 a fleet of cars pulls up. The first person I see is MacPherson, my cousin Mack's oldest son, unexpectedly up from Destin. A large, handsome man in his late twenties with prematurely gray hair, MacPherson as a toddler had regularly visited my parents after their retirement here. Unable to say "Lou Ellen," he had called my mother "Wella."

"MacPherson's here!" I announce.

Next up the ramp is a very tall, good-looking boy with dark hair and eyes. "I am Conrad," he says as we shake hands.

"Yes, you're the exchange student from Switzerland." He seems relieved to be expected.

He is followed by Braxton, Abe's middle child, whom I hug hello. Conrad watches, appearing happy to see his new host-brother get a hug and equally happy not to have gotten one himself. Nine-year-old Kathryn and Crum,

122

fourteen, Abe's other two children, escort in two of their cousin's on their mother's side—Hannah and her brother, Jim Bonner.

"Do they really call you Jim Bonner?" I ask.

"Sometimes we call him Jimbo," Hannah says.

Mildred, Johnny, Rose Mary and Miss Mendy arrive. Johnny makes the mistake of asking if I need any help, and I draft him and MacPherson into pouring lemonade. I give Kathryn the tasks of counting the people and putting the silver straws into the glasses, and she seems happy with both assignments. "Thirteen," she tells me a minute later.

Mildred wants me to show Conrad around the house and point out family pictures, but Crum volunteers to do it. "What year was this house built?"

"1838," I say.

MacPherson examines the gift I've brought Mother. "What kind of wood is this? It's funny...I know South American wood a lot better than I know American wood"

I have a minute to make small talk. I ask Braxton if he's playing football this year (he is) and if his brother Crum is any good on the guitar.

"He's pretty good," Braxton says.

"What kind of music is he playing?"

"A little of everything. Have you ever heard of Pink Floyd?"

I have.

Now it's a matter of split-second timing. I have to get Mother out of her chair and into the dining room, scoop thirteen dishes of ice cream and corral the guests into the dining room before the ice cream and the ice in the lemonade melt. I jam the two wax eights into the cake and begin feverishly scooping ice cream. My helpers have all absconded. I run lift Mother into the wheelchair and deposit her in the dining room. "MacPherson," I shout. "Would you put the lemonade around at the places?"

The explorers are rounded up and I ask Johnny to make sure that everyone has a chair and silverware. Somehow Conrad has managed to be the only one left standing. "Where do you want Conrad to sit?" Mildred asks.

"Wherever you can find him a place!" We have plenty of chairs. Mildred makes room for him by her at the end of the table.

Johnny lights the candles and I holler at Rose Mary, who is telling a long anecdote in Mildred's direction. The ice cream is melting in the sweltering heat, and I know from previous experience that it's only a matter of seconds before the candles go out. "Rose Mary!" I finally succeed in screaming her into submission. "Lead us in singing Happy Birthday!"

Conrad sings along, having apparently been clued in to this American custom. I hold the cake a few inches in front of Mother's face, and she manages to blow out both candles, to wild applause.

Then I slice the cake and begin frantically slapping it onto plates.

"Emily Jane, Conrad doesn't have a spoon," says Mildred.

This is the last straw. "Someone else is going to have to figure out what to do about that," I say. Right at this moment I can't do anything about it." Everyone else in the room is too old, too young or too male to be entrusted with the rapid service of cake and ice cream. "That's Johnny's job."

Despite being new to this woman's work, Johnny manages to find a spoon.

"I wished that I could walk again," Mother says. When she blew out the candles, she meant.

The table erupts into a flurry of consumption and conversation. "I said hello, how are you, in Spanish and she just looked at me like I was crazy," says MacPherson, talking about Nathalie. "I guess it must mean something different in Portuguese."

"Yeah, probably, 'I want to pierce your navel,'" I say to Johnny. He and Jim Bonner laugh. Nathalie's revealing outfit has been a hot topic all day.

"Personally, I don't think anyone should interfere with her cultural freedom to express herself," says Johnny.

Abe comes in, having stayed late at the funeral. I jump up to get him some ice cream and lemonade and come back to find Mildred in the middle of a joke: "...and the little boy said, 'My daddy's a stripper in a gay bar.'"

What? I have to hear this.

"And the teacher says, 'Son, I know that's not true. What does your daddy really do?' And the little boy cried and said, 'I just didn't want to say. My daddy works for Arthur Anderson.'"

The boys finish eating and resume their tour. At my end of the table I'm recounting the Ervy-Nervy-General Lee story from the day before: "...and I said, 'Isn't that an unusual name for a black child?'"

Abe and Johnny say in unison, "Our UPS man is named General Lee."

MacPherson comes in with the battered stock of an old rifle. "Hey! Isn't this a Civil War gun? Didn't Uncle Buddy blow it up?"

The answer to both questions is yes, but it was an accident. Buddy had just wanted to see if the gun would still shoot.

"They must have rambled through everything," Mother says. "That gun was in the back of a closet."

The boys are leaving to go fishing. Conrad shakes my mother's hand, and she tells him to visit any time. Johnny says, "Auf Wiedersehen."

Conrad backs out of the room, laughing.

"What name did the preacher use at the funeral?" Mildred asks Abe.

"He called him Doll Baby."

"The preacher didn't do that when Cousin Doodoo died. It was 'Henry Strudwick' this and 'Henry Strudwick' that. His sister said, 'I don't know who they just buried! My brother's name was Doodoo!'"

126

On that note we vacate the dining room in favor of the narrower, but cooler family room. Kathryn and her cousin Hannah set up the Chinese Checkers board. Kathryn says something to "Uncle Johnny" in passing.

"Hey, how do you rate being called an uncle? She called me 'Miss Emily!'" In actuality, we are both her second cousins.

Johnny tells about taking Allie to Birmingham for testing. "How can you really test the IQ of a two-year-old?" he asks me.

"I don't know. I think it has something to do with how fast they can put a raisin in a bottle, but I'm not sure how that translates into success in later life."

"I know she can put a raisin in a bottle," he asserts.

Rose Mary tells about the time Allie painted her entire body with lipstick when she visited for the weekend.

"Artistic talent," I say.

Johnny beams proudly.

The party is winding down. Hannah, with whom I have no kinship whatsoever, had heard my complaints about being called "Miss." Enacting the part of the perfect relative, she hugs me goodbye. "Goodbye, Aunt Betty," she says.

Later as I'm getting Mother ready for bed, she is musing not only on the events of the day, but on the last eighty-plus years. "It's been a wonderful day. Everything was just perfect...Frances looks more feeble to me. She's getting so stooped." She mentions a disreputable distant cousin who was Hugo Black's mistress. Mentioning him makes her think of the Ku Klux Klan. "My daddy never would join the Klan," she says. "At least not as far as I've ever heard."

"Mildred says the same thing," I respond. My grandfather having been the lone white male holdout in Arlington has been a source of pride to me.

I put the medicine in her eyes. "Doll Baby Wright lived in Pine Hill all his life, but I don't think I ever saw him," she says.

I never even *heard* of him.

In the morning I bring her breakfast and put all the dishes away. I get her cleaned up, but decide to leave her in bed until Shirley comes to relieve me at 10:00. At 8:30 I walk out to get the mail. I stop to brush Ginny Rai, my mother's sweet yellow porch dog, whose name derives from the concoction of gin and raisins much favored by the local ladies as a palliative for arthritis. Ginny Rai follows me happily to the Post Office.

A black man leaning on a cane is standing at the edge of the post office parking lot. We say good morning.

Box 296 is empty, but I hear the sounds of Carolyn, Arlington's first black postmistress, whom I've never met, still putting the mail in the boxes. I wait a minute and try the box again. "Good morning," I say through the wall.

"How's your mother doing this morning?" she asks.

Outside I see that Ginny Rai has settled in next to the man with the cane. "She thinks you're It today," I say.

"She know everybody," he replies.

Chapter fifteen

The Nettles Way

My brother called me from Nevada back in October, 2002 to give me a heads-up about Thanksgiving. It seemed that everybody (except him and my sister) was coming to my mother's house for Thanksgiving—somewhere in the neighborhood of sixty people—and that I was to be responsible for orchestrating the whole event. It was all Aunt Mildred's big idea (this much was true) but otherwise Mike was off by over 800%. There would only be ten of us for dinner. With Shirley, Lyda and Maggie Mae preparing certain key items (the dressing, sweet potatoes, pecan pies and marinated vegetables) in advance of my arrival from Nashville on Wednesday, it was considered doable. Yeah, right. I'm familiar enough with the drill to know that no matter what got done beforehand, the placement and heating issues alone would still turn out to be an insane amount of work. But I had been elected.

The climactic moment of the feast found me covered in whipped cream uttering expletives that are simply not used in my mother's kitchen (Shit! for example); but fortunately this explosion was witnessed only by John Cook, then aged twenty-three and himself no stranger to vice, and not by any of the innocent oldsters or Nicaraguans.

Certain other curse words (bastard, son of a bitch) are not only permissible in this company, but on special occasions are even required in the service of historical accuracy, as will later be made clear.

Since this was to be her first Thanksgiving as a resident of the United States, Mildred's youngest grandchild (Marianne Denise Cook-Chamorra) was to be treated to an exhibition of how our family does things—before Mildred, aged eighty-three, or my mother, eighty-eight, should happen, in the common parlance, to drop dead. Mildred wanted Marianne, the well-traveled bilingual five-year-old, formerly of Nicaragua and Peru, to experience a holiday feast with a Nettles, rather than a Dauphin, flavor—Nettles being Mildred and my mother's maiden name, Dauphin the maiden name of my cousin Abe's wife Helen, whose mother Maris would otherwise host the travelers, as she had done in years before.

Despite my treasonous ideas and Yankee ways, I was singularly qualified to perform this feat of southern hospitality by virtue of being one of only two granddaughters of Maude Rikard Nettles to have come down through the female line. My sister Nancy, the other one, was exempt due to being in Colorado. Mildred, who, as has been said, was the former President-General of the International United Daughters of the Confederacy is a southern matriarch *par excellence* and one who does not easily brook dissent. She is, however, extremely fun to tease.(Please humor me, if you will, in persisting in the present tense. It's all relative.)

Getting Started

At one-thirty on Wednesday afternoon I arrive at Mother's to find two adorable kittens, one yellow, one black, soaking up the sun on the back porch. These are the last of two sets of strays, the others having been previously eaten by marauding dogs. Cats here in Wilcox county are regarded as a form of miniature livestock, their primary function, inexplicably, seen to be the eradication of snakes. I have never seen a cat eat a snake in my life.

Growing up, we were allowed to have cats indoors, but back then we had basements in which to put a litter box, and my father was still alive. Despite his own Deep South origins, he was a strong proponent of indoor cats. The beautiful Kitty Tom, my sister's pick in Mclean, had always been first to arrive at our breakfast table in West Virginia, claiming his spot in my father's chair. Daddy would apologetically ask him to move over when he joined the table a few minutes later.

Shirley is elated by my arrival four hours earlier than promised, as it means she can go ahead and leave for Mobile to fetch her two-year-old grandbaby, Maude Lillian, who is the child of her husband Early's son by his first wife.

"That's certainly an old-fashioned name," I comment.

133

"I had a cousin with the same name, Lillian Maude," says Mother.

I'm confused. "I thought you said her name was Maude Lillian."

"Either way. They haven't decided yet," Mother claims. Shirley declines comment.

Before she leaves, Shirley demonstrates for me her cat protection device, a heavy wooden box on the porch, lined with paper and open at the top, into which she places the kittens at night. A metal tray is placed over the top, weighted down with a board. She leaves.

I heat a plate of leftovers for my lunch and immediately set about brewing three pots of tea, filling two sugar bowls, and slicing two lemons for Thursday's iced tea. I have brought rolls and material for mincemeat pie, as well as containers for the turkey broth I anticipate making on Friday. The oven lacks both a working thermostat and a timer, so I put Mother in charge of telling me when twenty minutes are up so I can check the pie. As she catches me up on the news, I begin making rings of aluminum foil with which to steady the ten yellow candles in the two silver candelabra. Mercifully, these have already been polished, though at some mutinous cost on the part of Shirley and Lyda, I suspect.

Mother asks me if I'm still going to visit the old people at the high rise, and I allow that I am.

"Are any of them cute?"

"They're all cute. They're just adorable." They're also all black. I refrain from elaborating

134

further on their cuteness, knowing it would just make her jealous.

"Johnny is already going with someone over in Camden, I hear."

"Who's he going with?"

"*A Henderson*! Daddy would roll over in his grave if he knew one of us had taken up with those Carpetbagger Hendersons...but at least they weren't Scalawags."

I press her for the distinction between a Carpetbagger and a Scalawag as I jump up to rescue the pie from incineration. She had forgotten to watch the clock. The pie is overly brown around the edges, but still appears to be edible. I pull the dressing and the sweet potato dishes out of the freezer to let them thaw out in the refrigerator, and start washing demitasse cups for the signature mulled grape juice.

We start a game of Scrabble. She complains that the bag for the tiles in the set that Nancy got at a yard sale (since the S's had rubbed off in the old set) is too small for her to comfortably reach into, but the old green bag in the other set is one she made thirty years ago, and it has been in almost continuous use since. It smells terrible. I tell her I'll wash it in the next load. As usual, she complains about Shirley's constant luck in drawing all the good letters: her refusal to abide by time limits: and her unfailingly fruitful search through the Scrabble dictionary. I help Mother find a seven-letter word (TALENTS) which allows her to win the second game. Though her joy in the victory is tainted by my help, this seems like a good place to stop.

She wants us to use the thin crystal tea and water glasses that have been collecting dust on a shelf in the pantry. All twenty of these must also be washed. A word on Mother's kitchen: there are approximately ten drawers and over forty doors, including those on cabinets, hutch and pie safe, and given the massive amount of material contained within and the fact that I've never lived in this house, my success in finding items on the first try is spotty at best. Among those things that need to be found: the wicker cornucopia to use as a centerpiece; Indian corn to hang on the door; the turkey roaster; the lemon juicer; lids to fit the saucepans...and here I'm just talking about what's in the kitchen.

In the dining room are four large pieces of furniture, including a china cabinet and a High Boy, in which hundreds, perhaps thousands, of items made of linen, silver, glass and china are either displayed or cleverly concealed. I've lucked out in the linen department, as the lace cloth is already on the table, and all I have to do is select ten napkins that are somewhat similar, and which display the proper L-shaped fold.

Mother starts worrying about when Laura Dell (really Laura Adele, nee Middlebrooks) will arrive from Montgomery. Laura, as she prefers to be called, is Mother's youngest first cousin. She has been a fixture at our holiday gatherings in recent years, as her own small family consists of one son who is far away, and one brother whom she boycotts because he is such an extremely Baptist minister. I've asked her to come tonight, if possible, so she can help with some of the fetching and setting. She arrives around six. I put a white linen cloth on the card table that is set up in front of Mother so we can eat supper here in lieu of me having to hoist her out of the chair and wheel her to the other table.

We have a charming supper of leftovers, courtesy of Shirley—chicken wings, meatloaf, rice, etc. Mother probes for any indication that Laura's male friend Pat might harbor matrimonial designs. She doesn't realize that Pat is gay.

Wasps and Prejudice

Laura entertains Mother as I grate onion into cream cheese to spread on crackers for hors d'oeuvres tomorrow, and doctor up some pimiento cheese I've found with habanera sauce and pepper. I open the silver chest on the window seat and count out knives, forks, salad forks, spoons and iced tea spoons in sets of ten. I dump these and a heap of serving utensils (lemon forks, pickle forks, jelly server, big spoons, meat forks, etc.) onto the dining room table. There are wasps buzzing around the tops of the lace curtains in both the living room and dining room. I try some ant and roach spray, but it doesn't spray high enough. This doesn't worry me much since wasps are usually fairly tractable this time of year.

I start boiling the turkey neck and gizzard for later use in giblet gravy, and count out ten china plates. The antique sauce boat I once gave Mother is required for the Jezebel sauce for the ham, and only the tall, stemmed Fostoria glass bowl can be used for cranberry jelly. I start amassing platters, vegetable bowls, relish dishes, bread trays, coffee cups and dessert plates. Most of these I have to wash.

It's time to put Mother to bed. This procedure involves removing clothing and teeth, lifting her out of the wheelchair and pulling a pair of stretch gloves over her twisted fingers so that her sensation of stickiness won't be so bothersome.

Laura Dell and I settle in to visit for a while. She's had a bad day. She rails about the incompetence of the administration of the Job Corps where she works as a counselor, irate that they waited until Wednesday to make a decision about when the students could leave for Thanksgiving, creating turmoil, fury and a massive amount of paperwork for her. "I know I'm prejudiced," says Laura, who grew up in Selma, "but it seems to me that these black administrators we've got are just unbelievably incompetent. Maybe it's just Southern blacks...but how can I say I'm prejudiced when my best friend there is black? And my last supervisor was black, and I loved him."

I decline to attempt to address the issue of Southern versus non-Southern blacks.

"And they all want us to call each other 'Ms.' and 'Mr.' —all our fellow employees. I think that must be a black thing, too. I can understand it when the students are around, but I know the people who wrote the policy never intended us to talk that way just among ourselves."

"I don't see what harm it does for students to call teachers by their first names, anyway," I say. "After all, you're trying to prepare them for the work place, and these days almost everybody goes by their first names."

"That's right! So I suggested to Rosa that she just call me Laura and let me call her Rosa...but she keeps on calling me 'Ms. Aubele.' And her being black, I really can't just keep calling her 'Rosa' if she's going to call me that."

"No, you really can't." The wasps are buzzing desultorily in one lime-green corner of the family room near the ceiling.

Laura is also distressed about the letter she received from her sister-in-law about her ardent hope for her salvation and her joy in her daily walk with Christ which she longs to share with her. Laura is furious at the intrusion, the holier-than-thou implications, and I tell her I would be, too, which relieves her. She had previously put in a clear request that her sibling and his spouse cease and desist from this kind of epistolary onslaught and her wishes are being ignored. She plans to not reply. Makes sense to me.

She says of her son, also a very committed Christian, but one who goes easier on the proselytizing (notwithstanding her membership in the Episcopal Church, which apparently doesn't count), "Johnnie still goes to see Billy and them, and he says, 'Mama, it's not like we just sit around and talk about Jesus the whole time.'"

"But they probably would if *you* were there,
"I remark as I take off my shoes and start rubbing
my feet, which are not accustomed to my
remaining vertical for such long periods of time.

It's late and I need to get up at four a.m. to
put the turkey, which weighs twenty pounds, in
the oven, so we go to bed—Laura in the front
blue bedroom, and me in the yellow room
between that one and Mother's. It's the
"daughters' room," a sort of prison, with no
independent door.

At four a.m. I get up and put the turkey into
the oven, setting the temperature at 325 degrees. I
pull the meat off the boiled neck to make the
gravy later, then go back to bed until six a.m.—at
which time I change Mother's diaper, help her
with her morning ablutions and bring her a
breakfast tray with a cinnamon roll, orange slices,
coffee, water and pills, and applesauce with
which to take them.

She wants to select a storybook for Lillian
Maude (or Maude Lillian) in case Shirley brings
her by on Friday, and she looks through a bag of
books she has on hand for such occasions. She's
in favor of *The Little Mermaid,* but I lobby for a
heavy cardboard book in the shape of a purse
which I think might help spare a black two-year-
old a too early indoctrination into the standards of
white girl beauty. At least the protagonists are
brown-skinned—though they comment on a need
for suntan lotion.

140

The Buildup

I dress Mother in her pale green two-piece Leslie Faye dress with the pearl and silver buttons, and array myself even more ornately in the green and gold outfit studded with pearls and beads and sequins that I had picked up off the ground at a yard sale for two dollars. (Have I mentioned that Bipolar Disorder is the family strain of mental illness? Lately I've suspected that I might be coming down with it.) Mother finds my elegant attire stunning.

The turkey is cooking way too fast, so I turn the unreliable thermostat down to 300, but by mid-morning it is so done that the meat is falling off the bone. My plan: reheat it thoroughly before serving time so as to kill off any bacteria that might incubate in the meantime.

Laura joins me in the kitchen and promptly burns up a cinnamon roll, which she dumps, still on its plate, into my pan of dishwater. Then she proceeds to blow up the microwave by trying it out with nothing in it. I had hoped to employ the microwave later in heating casseroles, and find myself getting just the tiniest bit testy.

After setting the table in the dining room, Laura entertains Mother by playing the piano, which does help. The tasks continue at a steady pace during the next few hours, and as I hunt behind the dozens of doors for the needed items, peel potatoes, rearrange the refrigerator and try to keep up with the annoyingly steady stream of things needing to be washed, I reflect upon the time a few years back when Mother lost her mind on Thanksgiving. It's easy to see how a thing like that could happen. I had been at home in Tennessee that year, and didn't get to sample the spectacular dish of nuttiness until the next day, after Uncle Buddy had interrupted my own Thanksgiving dinner to summon me down. "Emily Jane, your mama's gone insane and your daddy's going blind, and you need to get down here and see about it," he had tersely instructed me.

The immediate precipitants for Mother's first ever psychotic break seem to have been the failure of a guest to have made a fruit salad, as planned, topped by the horrifying realization as she checked the turkey close to showtime that it had been sitting for hours in an oven that had never even been turned on. She had gone start raving mad at that point, angrily lecturing hallucinated students from forty years earlier, then slyly assuring the troop of bemused holiday guests that she had arranged the whole thing as a test. A "priority test," she called it. She had grossly insulted a grandchild and a beloved nephew by attempting to enlighten them as to their respective supposed conditions of bastardy and moronity.

Today Mildred and her bunch are bringing a ham and a congealed salad, and while I am resigned to the idea that I will have to get the salad onto artfully arranged lettuce leaves on the proper etched glass plate (or maybe teach Claudina, Mack's teenaged stepdaughter to do it),

142

they better not be expecting me to slice that ham. It's an arduous job, especially with Mother's dull knives, and tends to keep one rooted in a particular spot while ten other things need doing.

Laura Dell assembles her green pea and asparagus casserole, and she requires a colander to drain the can of peas. I surmise that she may not do much cooking. I make the mulled grape juice (from memory, doubling it, as there is no recipe on hand), fill the celery chunks with pimiento cheese and start heating the sweet potatoes and dressing in the oven. I boil the "Irish" potatoes, but decide to wait to mash them. I get Laura Dell to spread the cream cheese on the crackers.

Around noon, the guests troop in. Mack eyes my glittering garb with a look of some askance. His own womenfolk are attired in a kind of collegiate chic.

"It's my Harem-Girl-Goes-to-Vegas outfit," I explain.

Mildred loves it.

It Begins

I draft Claudia, Mack's Nicaraguan second wife into pouring and serving the mulled grape juice in tiny cups, and put Laura Dell in charge of the hors d'oeuvres as I make the gravy and mash the potatoes. Mack, my tall handsome cousin three years my senior, has come blessedly prepared with an electric knife to slice the ham, and I give Claudina, aged sixteen, a crash course in the proper arrangement of congealed salad.

Mack is talking about the mahogany trade in Fiji and governmental corruption in Peru and Nicaragua as he slices the ham. It all sounds very interesting, but I'm slightly distracted as I mash the potatoes, stir the gravy and make sure everyone has what they need in the next room. John and MacPherson, Mack's sons from his first marriage, come in. I have the still-warm turkey sliced and covered on a plate, depriving Marianne Denise of the experience of watching the full fowl being dismembered at the table, but the turkey is so very tender that I know it would only fall apart if I tried to transfer it whole from the roasting pan. Enough is enough. I have put the cream in a bowl to whip at some unspecified intermission, after carefully reacquainting myself with the mechanism of the mixer.

It's time to get the tea and water poured, and to begin the process of getting Mother from her recliner to the dining room. Then everyone is seated but Laura, who has gone off somewhere, presumably to wash her hands. Mildred and Mother want the ten candles lit, though it is noon and sunny, and for this I have to find the matches. Mother has put Claudina, who is a new superstar in English, despite having only lived in Florida for six months, in charge of reading a psalm on thankfulness, and while I agree that this is an excellent idea, my internal timer is clicking away the moments that the rolls are spending in the oven—and before Claudina can read the selected

144

verses, Laura Dell first has to emerge from the nether regions of the house and Mildred has to finish what seems to be an extremely long story about how my great aunt Rubye (Rikard McWilliams) saved the family farm by taking charge when she was fourteen after her father died.

Rubye had gotten her twelve-year-old brother to hitch up the wagon, and had ridden into town to go to the bank, seeking a loan to buy the seeds for that year's crop. Her signature on the loan had been deemed a sufficient guarantee. (Note: Some thirty years later Rubye had become the first woman in Alabama to be elected to the office of tax collector—in Wilcox County, the poorest county in the United States, during the Depression. Unlike her fellow tax collectors in neighboring counties who profiteered at the time, she had determined that no one, white or black in Wilcox County would lose his land due to inability to pay taxes. She had paid the delinquent taxes herself out of her salary, and for the next forty years collected her repayment in the form of chickens, pecans and peaches, meticulously noted in her ledger.)

And Mother keeps clearing her throat to make some pronouncement of thankfulness until two or three of us succeed in leading Mildred's story to a close. Claudina, next to me, with her sleek, dark hair pulled back and her perfect English, begins at last to read the psalm, and I'm just itching to snatch that Bible out of her hands and return it to the living room while the food is still at some desired approximation of the right temperature for consumption, and before the rolls burn to a crisp.

The blessing at last having been accomplished, beautiful little Marianne gazes about in wonder. "Las abejas!" she exclaims.

"English, Marianne," Mack reminds her.

"Bees!" she says obediently, enthralled by the sight of wasps near the dining room ceiling.

I jump up to bring the rest of the stuff in, and ask Laura Dell to serve my plate and Mother's. There are pickled pears from Miss Mendy, homemade cranberry relish from Maris...way too many items even for a twenty-foot table. Everyone needs help in passing, serving, locating the right utensils, finding places to put things down. But the turkey is miraculously warm and tender, and Shirley's cornbread dressing is slightly chilly, but superb.

"I did have four kittens," Mother is saying, "but those old dogs killed them. They just ripped them apart."

Claudina seems on the verge of fainting with horror. "I didn't need to hear that," she says.

I cut up Mother's meat and butter her roll, managing to actually eat myself for nearly three continuous minutes before I have to go get her pills and applesauce. When my cousin Johnny, who is en route to a dinner in Birmingham, comes in to deliver a tin of pralines and say hello, I get up to whip the cream for the pies.

John Cook follows me in with a few plates. We talk about his job, helping to defend nursing homes from lawsuits. "I know it sounds terrible, like the nursing homes are the bad guys, but most of these suits are really bogus. These people sue who never even came to visit their relatives."

The mixer is plugged in, and all I have to do is turn it on. Big mistake. Cream flies instantly everywhere—over the counter, the floor, all over my festive get-up and my face. "Shit," I yell, and then again, along with other fervent expressions of dismay.

"I'll pretend I didn't see that," John offers gallantly, as he starts tearing up paper towels to help mop up. Claudia, too, comes in to help with damage control.

I swab myself off a bit, then reenter the dining room to explain the mishap to the guests. "Well, there's just not going to be any whipped cream," I announce.

"Then what will we put on the pie?" Mildred asks.

"*I don't know*," I say, with murderous calm. At this juncture I insist on snuffing out the ten candles, feeling certain that at the rate I'm going I might somehow manage to set myself on fire while serving coffee.

Mother tells of a similar experience in which she splattered whipped Jello all over the kitchen ceiling the day the Japanese attacked Pearl Harbor.

Two or three of the able-bodied set about clearing dishes, including my half-eaten plate of food. The coffee is ready. After a minute or two I relent and dig out the eggbeater. As I'm starting to whip the cream, MacPherson happens by and offers to help, so I make him do it. "I'm sorry that every time I see you I end up bossing you around," I apologize.

"That's okay, I'm used to it," he says. "After all, I *am* Mildred Cook's grandson."

Then I actually get to sit down and enjoy a piece of mincemeat pie with whipped cream, and a cup of coffee.

"Everything was perfect," says Mildred, innocently.

Conversation

I inquire of Claudina, to my right, as to her academic interests and plans.

"I think I want to be a journalist," she says.

"A dangerous job," I say.

"My mother was a journalist in Nicaragua," she reminds me. "And she says the same thing...'No! No!'" Claudia had been a television newscaster before the Contras took over. She was a Sandinista.

I compliment Claudina on her award in English. It was for a paper on *To Kill a Mockingbird*, she tells me. "I loved that book."

Mildred does not approve, even though Harper Lee was a local. "Around here we think her daddy wrote that book. She never wrote another one," she adds, incriminatingly.

I suspect that the book's indictment of southern racism might be another cause for Mildred's distaste. We finish our coffee and move to the living room, where the fire I lit hours earlier is still crackling merrily.

Mack is sitting in a rocking chair with Marianne snuggling in his lap; Claudia, Claudina and John are on the brocade sofa. The rest of us are in assorted platform rockers and chairs. Mildred launches into one of the tales about Cousin Doodoo, alias Henry Strudwick Nettles, who had married Elizabeth Agee sometime in the forties. These stories are always crowd-pleasers, even among non-native speakers of English. "And when the baby was born, Annie Mariah, their colored woman, asked Elizabeth what his name was. Elizabeth said, 'I named him Henry Strudwick, after his father.' And Annie Mariah said, 'Lord, Miss Elizabeth! I thought *Mr. Doodoo* was his daddy!'"

Claudia and Claudina collapse with laughter.

MacPherson asks a question about which of his forebears were Nettleses and which were Rikards. "It's the same family, MacPherson," I clue him in. "They kept marrying each other for generations. We're all related to ourselves in about six different ways."

Mother confirms that she is indeed her own third cousin.

"We're blue bloods," Mildred extrapolates.

"I believe the term is 'inbred,'" I observe.

But Mildred is sticking with blue blood, which reminds her of her genealogical coup. She has managed to uncover a connection between one of our ancestors and the illustrious Bluford family of Virginia. "There was a Thomas Nettles who was listed as being a caretaker for the Bluford bastards," she says proudly.

"The Bluford Bastards! That sounds like a football team," I say. Mildred's pride seems somewhat disproportionate to me, given that we're not even descended from the actual bastards—just from some kind of Bluford bastard babysitter. I muse upon how a family might collect all its illegitimate offspring in one spot to facilitate caretaking. Did they have their own wing of the house? Their own little bastard Christmas parties?

Mother mentions something about Uncle Sam.

"You mean the one who built the house on the hill?" MacPherson asks.

"No! That was *Brother*! Uncle Sam was my grandfather, Daddy's daddy. But we called him *Uncle* Sam because he was Mama's great-uncle."

"See what I mean?" I say to MacPherson.

John gets up to go outside to smoke and get some firewood.

"Mack and them have Tait blood in them from the Cook side," Mildred says. "A Tait will fight you." She tells the story about the Tait who shot his sister's bridegroom on the wedding day back in the 1840's. "...but it took him three days to die." That Tait had run off to Texas, a haven for fugitives in those days. "Back then there wasn't any law there," she explains. The man had gone on to become one of the preeminent citizens of Texas.

I begin to see an opening for a subject on which I'd like clarification.

Mildred continues: "And when Bragg met that girl in Atlanta whose mama was a Tait from Texas, Aunt Rubye said, 'I know exactly what Tait that is!'"

"I've been wondering," I say. "Did Papa Neil kill that man before or after his brother Jim killed the doctor?" I've been wondering about the sequence, and whether either murder had anything to do with my grandfather and his brother running off to Texas around the turn of the previous century.

"Dr. Whisenhunt," Mack injects. Marianne slides off his lap and slips away.

Mildred regards me blankly. "Daddy never killed anyone that I know of. That was Uncle Jim."

"Oh, come on. I've heard this all my life. Papa Neil was actually tried and convicted."

This still isn't ringing a bell with Mildred. She wants to tell the story of my great-uncle Jim's trial...how members of the governor's family had risen to his defense against the charge of murdering Dr. Whisenhunt. "It was ruled 'justifiable homicide.'"

"What was the justification?" I ask.

"The man called Uncle Jim a son of a bitch."

Hmm. Seems to me that a Tait is not the only one who will fight you.

And as for running off to Texas, Mildred is fuzzy on the subject. "They lived in Texas for a while when they were growing up."

"I know, but they were also there in about 1898. Papa Neil tried to enlist to fight in the Spanish-American War, but they wouldn't let him in the army because of his bad heart."

Mildred is befuddled. "How can that be? Uncle Jim got married in 1899...Cousin Bessie was born in 1900."

"Who knows?" I speculate. "Maybe even back then it took less than a year to get from here to Texas."

Despite herself, Mildred displays her usual good humor re the witticism.

Mack, however, has heard a little something about our grandfather committing a murder. "But it was just over a pair of shoes, so it doesn't really count."

"I heard it was over a white woman," I say.

Mother, too, claims ignorance.

"Oh, come on! You told me this yourself, when I was nine! He was on probation for a year, working under that doctor." (Another doctor.)

At last something clicks, and Mother begins to expound upon how much Dr. Kimbrough, my maternal grandfather's probation officer, had loved and admired her daddy.

"But why did he kill that man? And was it before or after Uncle Jim shot Dr. Whisenhunt?" I persist.

"It was after," Mother says. "It was a colored man." As if that is explanation enough.

"Oh, if it was just a *colored* man..." MacPherson says, directing this to me.

The irony is lost on Mother. The subject is closed.

Marianne comes in clutching the yellow kitten. Claudia, bless her, gets up and washes all of the dishes. Claudina and her stepbrothers tease each other.

The party in the living room creaks and crackles to a close. John and MacPherson leave to go hunting. I pack up bags of food for Laura Dell and Mildred to take home. The paper turkeys from the table are given to Claudina and Marianne.

"It's been a perfect, perfect day," Mildred sighs, with satisfaction.

Remember the Kittens?

Later I put the kittens to bed in their fortress, weighting down the top with a board and a brick. During the night there is a loud crash and the baying of dogs. In the morning the lid is off the box and the black kitten is missing. The tiny yellow kitten is up a tree, mewing piteously. I lure him down and carry him inside.

The yellow kitten, whose name is Friday, is unusually tame and affectionate for a porch cat. Throughout the day, as I boil the turkey bones for soup, I keep bringing him inside, hoping to reintroduce Mother to the joys of truly having a pet. The kitten purrs in her lap as we play Scrabble, then perches on her shoulder, watching with great admiration as she eats a piece of celery. I regret that my camera stopped working after the second shot yesterday at the table. Mother says the kitten can't be allowed to sleep inside...Shirley and Lyda would never permit it.

We watch in vain for Maude Lillian, who never comes, but in the late afternoon John, Jim and Debbie Lavender stop by. This is the first Thanksgiving since Aunt Jane, Mother's youngest sister, died, and Uncle John seems dazed with grief.

I make a decision. "I'm disobeying you," I announce to Mother, enlisting Jim's aid in dragging in the heavy box, lined with papers. It's not like Mother can get up and stop me, and I've about had it with the wanton destruction of cats around here. I figure that even if I weight the top down with a cinder block, those dogs would still be clawing at the box, barking and slobbering, and the kitten would likely die of fright. Even though there's no litter box, it seems to me that if the kitten could pee in the box outside at night, it can do the same thing in the house.

So Friday sleeps inside on Friday night. In the morning I put him outside for a while as I give Mother her breakfast in bed, then bring him back inside to nap beside her on the pillow as I get ready to leave. Shirley calls to say she's on her way and that I can go ahead and leave and she'll let herself in.

"Mom's got herself a kitten now," I say, and I tell her about the black one getting killed. I explain to her my reasoning regarding bringing the box inside. "Ginny Rai was devastated." I embellish, playing upon her fondness for the dog.

154

"She almost refused to go to the Post Office with me yesterday. She seemed to think she needed to stay and protect the kitten."

After I get back to Nashville and retrieve my own cat from the vet's, where he's been boarded, I call down there to see what the verdict is. I have to press Shirley for specifics. "Are you going to let the kitten stay inside?" Compared to most down there, Shirley counts as an animal lover.

"I've already put that box back out on the porch."

"But those dogs will scare him to death."

"We'll see," she laughs.

Epilogue

So that's it. End of story. And just as any character could have been chosen to commence, say that ancient unmentioned progenitor who established Rikard's Mill, there could have been any ending. My own emancipation, perhaps, or subsequent repatriation. Mother's death in 2004.

Who were the good guys? Who were the bad guys in this black-white checkered tale? Who won? It's not always so easy to say, now, is it? I myself could vie for villain, having had the rank audacity to pen (and I mean pen) this exposé. A note of moral ambiguity seemed a useful one to sound at this particular point in history.

Why this? It's what I got, just what I managed to hold onto, like the memory of the swing set and the invisible flying squirrel. It's a glass of juice distilled in part from those persimmons of recitation of what was whose great-uncle's mother's maiden name that my cousins and I were fed before we jumped up and went outside to run around and around and around on the exposed roots of the old magnolia tree.

Why now? Well, for one thing, I wanted to wait until Mildred died both to spare her sensitivities and stave off her editorial interference. And I was getting sick of that blustering blowhard who so dominates our airwaves and decided to instead turn on a private show. And then to broadcast it, since there is absolutely nothing I would put past him: not hiding as long as possible what is going on in the detention centers; not stopping the mail and blocking internet and press. It seemed a propitious (perhaps last) opportunity to dig those boxes of paper out from under my bed and start patching things together in the hope of finding, saving, a coherent whole.

This is a reach—hello, goodbye? most especially to my compatriots on the other side of the aisle. Oh, the Baptists love the Methodists, will the circle be unbroken down by the Green River in the land of the free.

Acknowledgements

This work was first typed directly onto Facebook from handwritten and old typed pages during the Covid-19 pandemic shutdown, between the dates of April 8 and April 17, 2020. Had it not been for the readers of the daily installments—cousins, colleagues, Scrabble buddies, old friends from George Washington High and elsewhere—who offered encouragement and egged me on, it is doubtful whether the project would have been brought to completion. I particularly appreciate the efforts of my old friend Melanie Foster Taylor and my cousins Mary Jane Nettles and John Nettles for collecting the pieces into files and sending them back to me. Without Katya Lezin, who also offered information about self-publishing, I might not have ever divined that the "enter" key also meant "return." I appreciate my second cousin Laura Aubele giving permission to include material more personal than the rest.

I would like to thank Dr. Melanie Foster Taylor for her patient instruction in how to deal with files, and Dr. Frances Page Glascoe for designing the cover and making an inspired choice for the author's photo, as well as assisting with the arcane niceties of publication. Both of them are sharp-eyed editors.

I thank my parents, Lou Ellen and Bill Griffin (yes, y'all, he really went by Bill, at least since 1953) who provided me with a life of opportunity and privilege, and spared me all the hideous forms of abuse to which I have borne witness almost daily throughout my working life. I am grateful that my brother, Mike Griffin, was never mean to me other than calling me a moron. I appreciate the many happy times and wonderful holidays with my ex-husband, Philip Brodeur, even in the years after our divorce.

I especially acknowledge my sister, Nancy Griffin Brown. She was my first friend and translator, my separated twin, my partner in the fabulous forgotten Shrinking and Growing Machine. Big sister turned to little sister, little sister back to big. We did that all our lives.